CW01418325

Stefano Biancalana and Michele M
updating by Giorgio Sarti

Vespa
From Italy with Love

GIORGIO NADA EDITORE

Giorgio Nada Editore s.r.l.

Editorial coordination
Antonio Maffeis

Cover and layout
Giorgio Nada Editore

Translation
Antony Shugaar

Illustrations
Fondazione Piaggio
Roberto Donati
Museo Nazionale del Ciclo e Motociclo, Rimini
Archivio Giorgio Sarti
Archivio Giorgio Nada Editore

Acknowledgements
The publisher would like to thank all those who have con-
tributed to the production of this book with photographic and
documentary materials.
In particular:
Archivio Storico Piaggio (Pontedera)
Roberto Donati
Museo Nazionale del Ciclo e Motociclo, Rimini

© First english edition, 2000 Giorgio Nada Editore,
    Vimodrone (Milan)

Printed in Italy

All rights reserved.
Apart from any fair dealing for the purpose of
private study, research, criticism or review, no
part of this publication may be reproduced, stored
in a retrieval system, or transmitted, by any
means, electronic, electrical, chemical,
mechanical, optical photocopying, recording or
otherwise, without prior written permission. All
enquiries should be addressed to the publisher:

Giorgio Nada Editore
Via Claudio Treves,15/17
I - 20090 VIMODRONE (MI)
Tel. +39 02 27301126
Fax +39 02 27301454
E-mail: nadamail@work-net.it
http://www.giorgionadaeditore.it

The catalogue of Giorgio Nada Editore
publications is available on request at the
address above.

Vespa: From Italy with love
ISBN: 88-7911-222-8

CONTENTS

Vespa

from Italy

with love

THE DREAM

TWO WHEELS JUST AS GOOD AS FOUR

Half a century after its inception, the Vespa remains an unrivalled legend, a myth that even today stands alone.

Its singularity is not merely technical (in the past half century, many improvements and innovations have been made, but the basic concept is unchanged) nor is it historical (the fundamental idea of the scooter is older than the Vespa, and dates back to the turn of the twentieth century). The truly unique dimension of the Vespa is social, and has much to do with its role as a catalyst for societal change. The Vespa is, technically, an industrial product, but in a much more profound sense it is a product of a changing lifestyle. The Vespa managed to personify the dreams of an entire society, and in so doing it served as a mental hinge; the Italians used the Vespa as a vehicle for their idea of the future, and the Vespa was the hinge of a door that opened the way for an entire society to join the modern world. And along with Italian society, it brought millions of others around

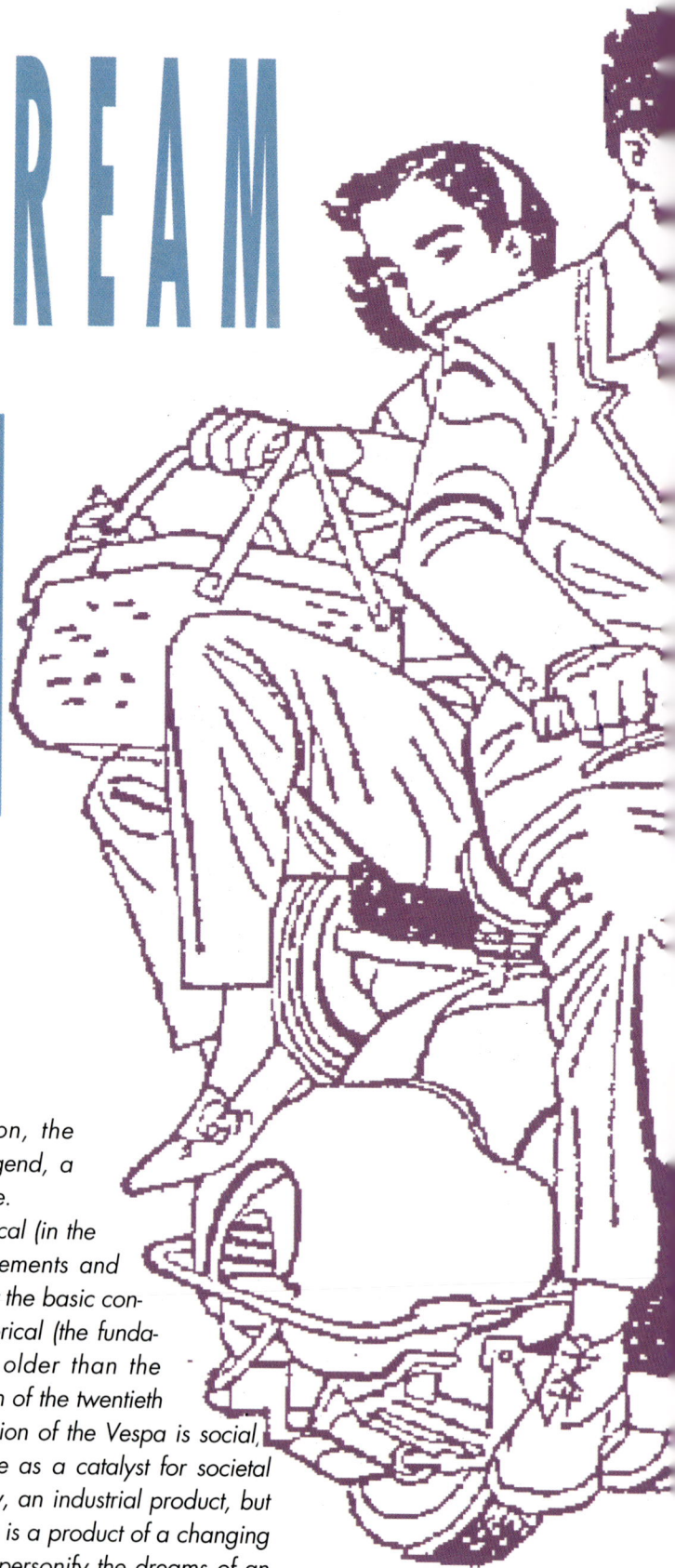

AFTER THE SECOND WORLD WAR, THE VESPA REPRESENTED THE MOST AFFORDABLE MEANS OF TRANSPORTATION FOR ITALIAN FAMILIES. IN A FEW YEARS, THE ROADS OF ITALY—STILL RAVAGED FROM RECENT COMBAT—BEGAN TO FILL UP WITH THESE INNOVATIVE LITTLE SCOOTERS. THE VESPA WAS EVERYWHERE, READY TO PERFORM THE MOST CHALLENGING TASKS THAT THE COLLECTIVE IMAGINATION OF THE ITALIANS COULD COME UP WITH.

the world into the modern world. There are those who look at the specific social context in Italy following the Second World War and limit the importance of the Vespa's role, saying that it was little more than a surrogate for the automobile in an underdeveloped society; as such, it was a compromise rather than an achievement. To quote from Aesop's Fables, and specifically the tale of the fox and the grapes: unable to reach a tempting bunch of succulent grapes that dangled high above its snapping jaw, a frustrated fox turned on its hindquarters and stalked off, saying that it didn't like grapes in the first place, and besides they were probably sour. The Vespa as the signal of a repressed desire, awaiting only better times and affordable automobiles? Hardly. The Italians were sick and tired of waiting for better times, and they had already spent twenty years drinking ersatz coffee (made from barley) and foregoing other luxuries and niceties. To persuade them to buy a scooter instead of a car would not have been a simple matter. And the Italians didn't even really possess an automotive culture in those years; the idea that everyone might own a car was not a common one. Even the Fiat Topolino, popular though it might have been, was still considered by most people to be a major "investment" (the Fiat 500 B cost 660,000 lire, equal to the price of six Vespas). Indeed, it would be ten more years before the Italians really decided on a mass level that the time had come to buy a car, with the Fiat 600. Long before that, the Italians had dreamt of the Vespa, as a scooter, for itself, not as a surrogate for some other consumer product. They loved the Vespa as it was, affordable, easy, practical, handy (for men and women). This friendly and original little vehicle had many virtues: it was frugal (it was cheap and it cost very little to run and maintain), it was immensely functional, it could adapt to any and all situations—all typically Italian qualities.

The Vespa was thus never a would-be automobile; indeed, it was from the outset a true car, albeit a very unusual one. Little did it matter that it had only two wheels, since it performed the exact same service as any four-wheeled automobile. In order to understand the reason for its success, suffice it to say that the Vespa was the right vehicle that pulled up at just the right time.

Engine: horizontal two-stroke single-cylinder, 98 cc. displacement, 3.2 hp at 4,500 rpm, Dell'Orto TA2 16/17 carburetor, three-speed gearbox, lubrication with 6 percent mixture, top speed 60 kph.

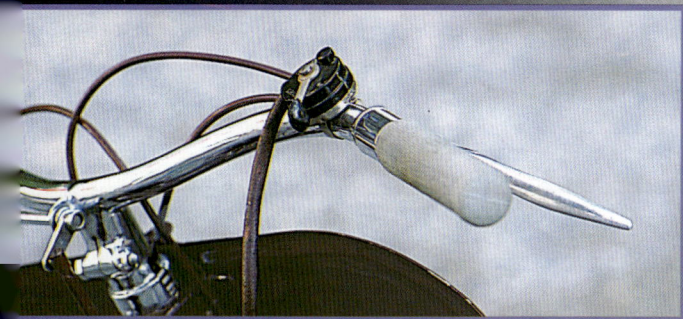

THIS WAS THE FIRST VESPA: THE CHEERFUL LITTLE 98. THE YEAR WAS 1946. IN THE WAKE OF THE WAR, ITALY WAS STRUGGLING TO GET BACK ON THE ROAD, AND THE FIRST RIDE WAS ON THE SADDLE OF A SCOOTER. THE VERY FIRST PIAGGIO VESPA WAS PRESENTED IN THE MONTH OF APRIL AND WAS EVEN BLESSED BY CARDINAL SCHUSTER OF MILAN. AT FIRST, MOST EXPECTED THAT THE VEHICLE WOULD FACE AN UPHILL ROAD, AS IT WERE, WITH ITS OPEN FRAME THAT ELIMINATED THE TRADITIONAL KNEE-SUPPORT OF THE GAS TANK, SMALL WHEELS, THE ABSENCE OF THE TRESTLE STAND, AND A DRIVE TRAIN AND MECHANICAL ARRAY THAT SEEMED A LITTLE TOO FRAGILE. INSTEAD...

THE DESIGN

FROM A DUCK TO A WASP

T

he product of brilliant intuition, the kernel of the idea that would develop into the Vespa began to form in early 1945 when war was still raging along the Italian peninsula. That was the year, in fact, that Enrico Piaggio decided it was time to change, in order to keep pace with times that were certainly about to change. As we would say nowadays, he knew that he had to reconvert his company, get ready to abandon the field of aeronautics (the manufacturing base for Piaggio) and invent something new: one good idea would be to develop a cheap and practical means of transportation that would help the country to get moving again after the stagnation that had been imposed by the Second World War.

An engineer named Vittorio Casini, entrusted with the project and working in Biella with another engineer named Renzo Spolti, built the first prototype for a Piaggio scooter, dubbed the MP5, and immediately renamed the Paperino (Italian for little duck, and also the Italian name of the Disney character, Donald Duck). This was a classically conceived scooter with direct drive, no gearbox, a tunnel-frame made of stamped sheet metal, a centrally mounted Sachs engine

ENGINEER CORRADO D'ASCANIO (BORN POPOLI, 1891—DIED PISA 1981), DESIGNER OF THE VESPA, AT HIS DESK. RIGHT, A MEMO SENT TO HIM ON 2 DECEMBER 1945 BY A COLLEAGUE, INFORMING HIM THAT THE MP6 PROTOTYPE WAS DISPLAYING CERTAIN ENGINE PROBLEMS WHEN OPERATING UNDER STRAIN. THE LETTER WAS SENT FROM BIELLA WHERE THE PIAGGIO COMPANY HAD MOVED ITS OPERATIONS DURING THE WAR, ON THE ORDERS OF THE RETREATING GERMANS.

Biella 2/12/45

Sig. Ing. D'Ascanio

Si stanno proseguendo le prove della MP.6, attualmente unico problema è il raffreddamento poiché da rilievi fatti con la normale copertura del motore risulta che su strada leggermente in salita la temperatura sale rapidamente oltre i 300° ed è necessario fermare per lasciare raffreddare.

È stato rilevato che l'ingresso dell'aria si trova in una zona che l'aria è quasi ferma per effetto dello scudo, mentre la corrente passa a ~ 10 cm discosta.

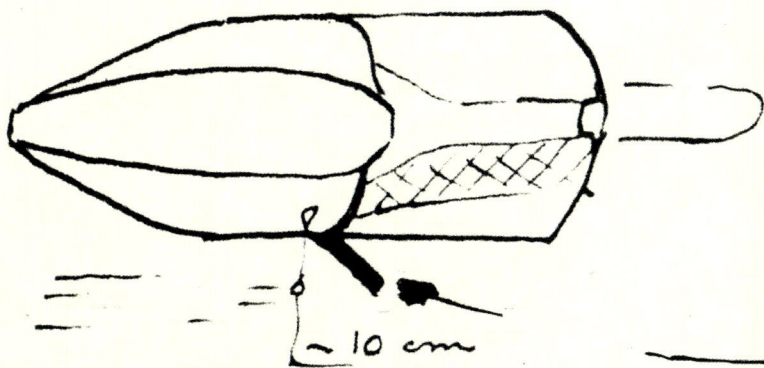

~ 10 cm

tegolo per convogliare aria

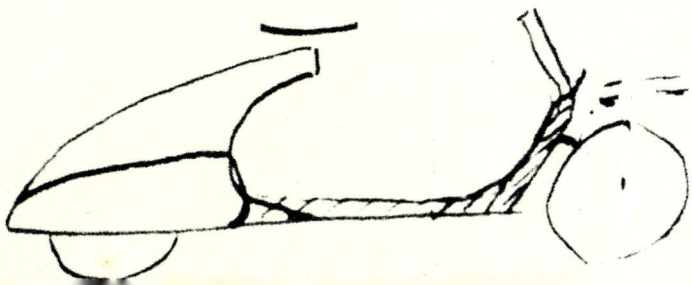

11

that was entirely enclosed by the bodywork, and a front shield that extended down and around to the running board. This initial design, however, did not meet with the approval of Enrico Piaggio, who clearly wanted something more revolutionary and innovative. Looking for a better solution, he commissioned an engineer from Abruzzo, Corradino D'Ascanio (already a successful aeronautical designer) to redesign entirely the scooter project, hoping for something more credible and appropriate.

And so the ugly duckling (Paperino) flourished and grew into a handsome swan, just like in the fairy tale by Hans

ENRICO PIAGGIO, SHOWN ABOVE WITH THE VESPA GS (1963). HE WAS DISSATISFIED WITH THE FIRST SCOOTER BUILT BY ENGINEER RENZO SPOLTI. IN HIS OPINION, THE PROTOTYPE, DUBBED MP5 BUT IMMEDIATELY NICKNAMED THE PAPERINO (ITALIAN FOR LITTLE DUCK, AND ALSO THE ITALIAN NAME OF THE DISNEY CHARACTER, DONALD DUCK), WAS NOT SUFFICIENTLY ORIGINAL. HE THEREFORE DECIDED TO COMMISSION THE ENGINEER CORRADO D'ASCANIO TO DEVELOP AN ALTERNATIVE IDEA. D'ASCANIO WAS A RESPECTED DESIGNER OF AIRPLANES AND HELICOPTERS, AND TRANSFERRED HIS AERONAUTIC EXPERIENCE TO THE NEW VEHICLE, DEVELOPING AN ABSOLUTELY REVOLUTIONARY AND UNPRECEDENTED PRODUCT.

Christian Andersen—or at least into a Vespa (Italian for 'wasp'), a name that came from the "buzzing" sound of its small new 98 cc. engine. D'Ascanio had come up with an original new vehicle (dubbed the MP6), based on features that were more typical of automobile than motorcycle manufacturing. Indeed D'Ascanio had studied motorcycles more with a view to identifying "the defects in terms of practical use" that kept them from reaching the mass market and had limited them to a narrow group of aficionados. Moreover, D'Ascanio had never been a "motorcyclist," nor had he even designed motorcycles professionally. All he knew about motorcycles was what they looked like; and he didn't think that they would appeal to a vast audience. Therefore, when he set to work to design a new motorscooter, he had a mindset that was unburdened with old conceptions and free of the standard approach to two-wheeled motor vehicles. He was determined to design a means of transportation that was intuitive and satisfying to people who had never

ridden a motorcycle. In this early conceptual phase of the design process, Corradino D'Ascanio established a few basic anchoring points. In his view, the new vehicle would have to possess certain minimum standards of comfort, which he listed in a series of four absolute "musts."

First: a flat tire should not mean a problem that can only be solved by a mechanic, and the rider should be able to change tires just like on a car.

Second: it should be easy to straddle and mount the vehicle (which led the designer toward a structure reminiscent of a woman's bicycle).

Third: because it should be supremely agile and maneuverable in city traffic, the vehicle should be simple to operate and steer, which meant that controls should be arranged so that the rider never has to take his or her hands from the handlebars.

Fourth: "So that clothing shall not be stained or damaged, the engine should be far away and isolated from the rider, and possibly enclosed."

This last requirement, along with the Pirelli company's inability to supply transmission belts of sufficiently high quality to ensure excellent and reliable operation (rubber was one of the hardest-to-find materials following the war) led to the decision to locate the gearbox and the engine over the rear wheel; the direct drive and the in-line gearbox made it possible to create a compact engine-wheel assembly that is even today one of the Vespa's outstanding features.

D'Ascanio derived many other technical features directly from his own and Piaggio's years of experience in the field of aeronautics, and so, as the engineer himself later wrote: "For several fundamental solutions on the Vespa, I took inspiration from various aeronautic approaches with which I was familiar, such as for instance the monotube support of the rear wheel [...]. As far as the frame was concerned, I found myself working well beyond the most modern automotive concepts, because the sheet-metal bodywork also served as frame, and because of its special manufacturing it provided even greater strength and resistance than the old tube-based system. Here too my experience in the field of aeronautics helped me; in that field the lightness of a structure must not interfere with its sturdiness."

Out of this interesting array of ideas, D'Ascanio, with the assistance of his trusted designer Mario D'Este, finally developed a vehicle that was revolutionary in every sense of the term. Practical, inexpensive, and therefore capable of helping an Italy that was still quite poor but was certainly not insensitive to the charms of beautiful things to get on the road. And unquestionably the Vespa, one of the best known symbols of Italian design, was a beautiful thing. Still, the project needed a name. As we have said, the name that was chosen was "Vespa," or 'wasp.'

.... and the story began.

THE PIAGGIO MP6 PROTOTYPE. THE NAME VESPA, OR 'WASP,' WAS SUGGESTED BY THE PARTICULAR BUZZING NOISE OF THE ENGINE, BUT ONLY CAME LATER. TOP, THE PHOTOGRAPH OF THE PROTOTYPE THAT WAS PRESENTED TO THE PRESS.

The first "official" act was the presentation of the new "Vespa runabout light-motorcycle" at the Rome Golf Club, with a guest of honor, the American General Stone, representing the Allied military occupation government. The event was filmed by the American movie news service, Movietone. And so, even before the Italians got a glimpse of it, the Vespa was before the eyes of the American movie-going public. Italians, on the other hand, had to settle for the black-and-white still photograph that appeared, on 15 April 1946, on the cover of "La Moto" magazine. After the first step had been successfully completed, it seemed that the second step would be considerably more difficult.

For the Piaggio company, breaking into the motorcycle market with the Vespa entailed a broad array of problems. First off, just how should Piaggio distribute a product that was so different from the range of products manufactured up to that time? How could Piaggio bring the Vespa to the mass market when its marketing structure was long accustomed to working only with a few select clients, all of whom were institutional in nature? The company's old clients were the Italian railway adminstration, foreign railways, governments and agencies that needed special vehicles. An extremely idiosyncratic clientele, therefore, that could be reached only through special channels.

The Vespa, on the other hand, was a product designed for a far broader and more fragmented market. It was therefore necessary to invent an entirely new distribution network, revolutionary for the Piaggio company. Moreover, adequate advertising support was needed. And so the company set to work on these new challenges as well, overcoming the handicap of inexperience with a considerable show of courage. The first distribution network for the Vespa in fact had some rather unusual features, which

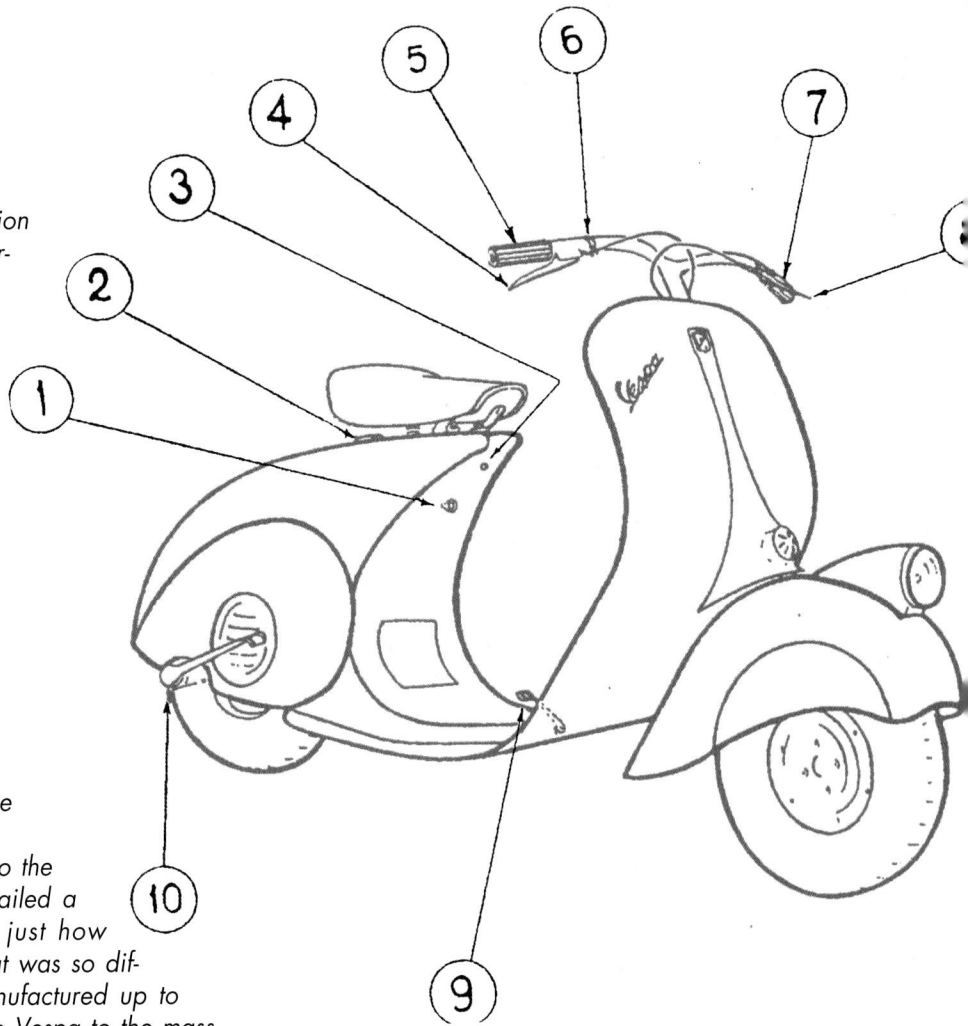

THE VESPA MADE ITS OFFICIAL DEBUT AT THE MILAN FAIR OF 1946. AT THE PIAGGIO STAND, EVEN THE ARCHBISHOP OF THE CAPITAL OF LOMBARDY, CARDINAL SCHUSTER, STOPPED TO EXAMINE THE INTERESTING NEW PRODUCT. IN THE PHOTO AT FAR RIGHT, A GLIMPSE OF THE PIAGGIO WAREHOUSE, IN PONTEDERA, 1952. THE PRODUCTION OF THE SCOOTER HAD ALREADY EXTENDED TO INCLUDE THE LARGER "APE" (ITALIAN FOR 'BEE') AND "MOSCONE" (OR 'BUMBLEBEE') OUTBOARD MOTORS.

entailed some cutting-edge decisions; its first introduction to the mass market was entrusted entirely to a specially organized company: SARPI (Società Agenzie Rappresentanze Prodotti Industriali, literally 'company of agents and representatives of industrial products'). This was a small Florence-based firm that Enrico Piaggio had purchased in that period, and which looked like the right solution to the problem.

There still remained a second obstacle to be overcome: how to organize thorough nationwide retail distribution of the new product? The decision was made to approach a company that already had a well-tested network in operation in this field. The first approach was to the Guzzi company. It would appear that, at the time, as long as he could find a distribution network, Enrico Piaggio would even have been willing to market his new scooter under the Mandello del Lario firm's name. After an initial series of promising contacts, however, the deal fell through. The management at Guzzi felt that the Vespa was a product without a future. And so Piaggio was forced to build a distribution network of its own, perhaps based upon an existing network that was less blind to the future than Guzzi. The company decided to sound out the terrain. The way that the engineer Barnato (shareholder in SARPI and perhaps the man who did most to shape the image of the Vespa) tells it, the Vespa's first contact with the market was fairly adventurous; Piaggio executives went around, practically door-to-door, with photographs of the Vespa, paying calls on Lancia automotive showrooms (they had decided to approach Lancia because they felt that the name would shed a dusting of class on the new scooter). Each of the car salesmen was asked to commit to a certain minimum number of Vespas. The idea worked.

According to some witnesses, this first round of contacts

TOYMAKERS IMMEDIATELY SEIZED THE OPPORTUNITY TO MANUFACTURE MODELS OF THE VESPA, AND THEY SOLD QUICKLY EVERYWHERE. HERE WE SEE TWO TOYS MADE BY INGAP IN 1955. ON THE FACING PAGE, A SKETCH OF THE CONTROLS AND EQUIPMENT OF THE VESPA 125, ALSO PRESENT ON THE 98 CC. MODEL.
1. RESERVE TANK LEVER.
2. FUEL CAP.
3. IGNITION SWITCH.
4. FRONT BRAKE.
5. THROTTLE GRIP.
6. HORN AND LIGHTS.
7. GEAR SHIFT.
8. CLUTCH LEVER.
9. BRAKE PEDAL.
10. STARTER PEDAL.

produced contracts sufficient to persuade the Piaggio company to plan a first production run of 7,500 units. Later, however, the sales of the first fifty Vespas to the public actually proved fairly problematic. This initial difficulty soon passed, however, and by the end of 1947 production began to climb, and with the presentation of the 125 model, the Vespa had firmly established itself. Particularly appropriate (considering the general shortage of ready cash) was the idea of offering the Vespa on the installment plan. In 1948, for instance, the Vespa 125 was offered to the public at a list price of 168,000 lire (plus 5,000 lire of IGE, a sales tax); if you paid cash there was an advance deposit of 50,000 lire (plus 1,500 lire of IGE) and the remaining 121,500 lire upon delivery. The scooter however could also be purchased on the installment plan with payments spread out over anywhere from 10 to 24 months (later, extended to 30 months). This sales mechanism made it possible to take delivery of a Vespa immediately by paying a very small advance deposit and then extending payment over a series of monthly notes. After overcoming this problem, the Pontedera-based firm had to deal with the problem of advertising. It was necessary to create immediately a suitable image to go with the new product. Here too the matter was not a simple one. The Vespa was something totally new, too new to hope to rely upon the usual means of communication. It was necessary to come up with a good idea.

In the end, the idea developed...

15

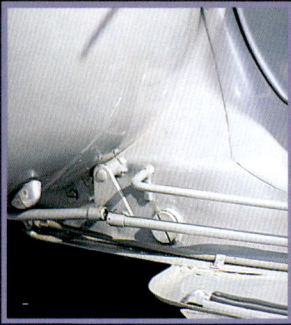

Engine: horizontal two-stoke single-cylinder, 98 cc. displacement, 3.2 hp at 4,500 rpm, Dell'Orto TA17 carburetor, three-speed gearbox, lubrication with 6 percent mixture, top speed 60 kph.

After a year of production, a few minor esthetic and mechanical modifications were made to the Vespa. One new optional extra was a little sheet-metal luggage rack, behind the seat; if necessary, it could be transformed into a passenger seat. Other modifications affected the starter pedal, the rear brake pedal, and the seat itself and its mounts. The engine was the durable 98 cc. model, which could reach a top speed of 60 kilometers per hour. It was much sought-after. In order to meet the demand, everyone at the plant had to work overtime!

98
1947

Engine: horizontal two-stroke single-cylinder, 124.85 cc. displacement, 4.5 hp at 4,500 rpm, Dell'Orto TA17 carburetor, three-speed gearbox, lubrication with 6 percent mixture, top speed 70 kph.

THE YEAR 1949 MARKED THE DEFINITIVE CONSECRATION OF THE VESPA 125. IN APPEARANCE, IT MIRRORED THE LINES OF THE 98, BUT THERE WERE SOME DIFFERENCES: ASIDE FROM ENGINE DISPLACEMENT AND PERFORMANCE, THE INTRODUCTION OF REAR SUSPENSION. THERE WAS ALSO A VARIATION IN THE FRONT SUSPENSION WITH THE WHEEL (STILL OFFSET) ON THE LEFT OF THE STEERING COLUMN INSTEAD OF THE RIGHT. THE ENGINE COMPARTMENT, HINGED AT THE TOP, WAS EASIER TO OPEN. THE METAL LUGGAGE RACK BECAME A STANDARD FEATURE, AS DID THE FUEL KNOB, WHICH NOW HAD A "RESERVE" SETTING.

125 UTILITARIA

So that "everyone" could now have the satisfaction of owning a Vespa, the Pontedera firm presented a new model, the 125 U, the 'U' standing for Utilitaria, or 'runabout.' The new model was extremely simple, but still resembled the standard version, while costing a good twenty thousand lire less. For the first time, the new Vespa Utilitaria featured a major cosmetic innovation: the headlight was high up on the handlebars, which had never been seen on Italian models, but had been featured on export models for some time.

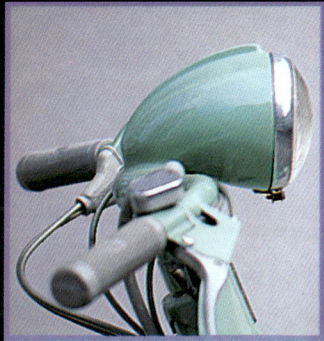

Engine: horizontal two-stroke single-cylinder, 124.85 cc. displacement, 4.5 hp at 4,500 rpm, Dell'Orto TA17 B carburetor, three-speed gearbox, lubrication with 5 percent mixture, top speed 65 kph.

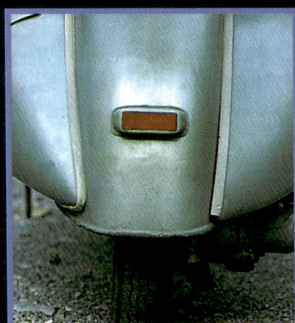

Engine: horizontal two-stroke single-cylinder, 124.85 cc. displacement, 4.5 hp at 4,500 rpm, Dell'Orto TA17 B carburetor, three-speed gearbox, lubrication with 6 percent mixture, top speed 70 kph.

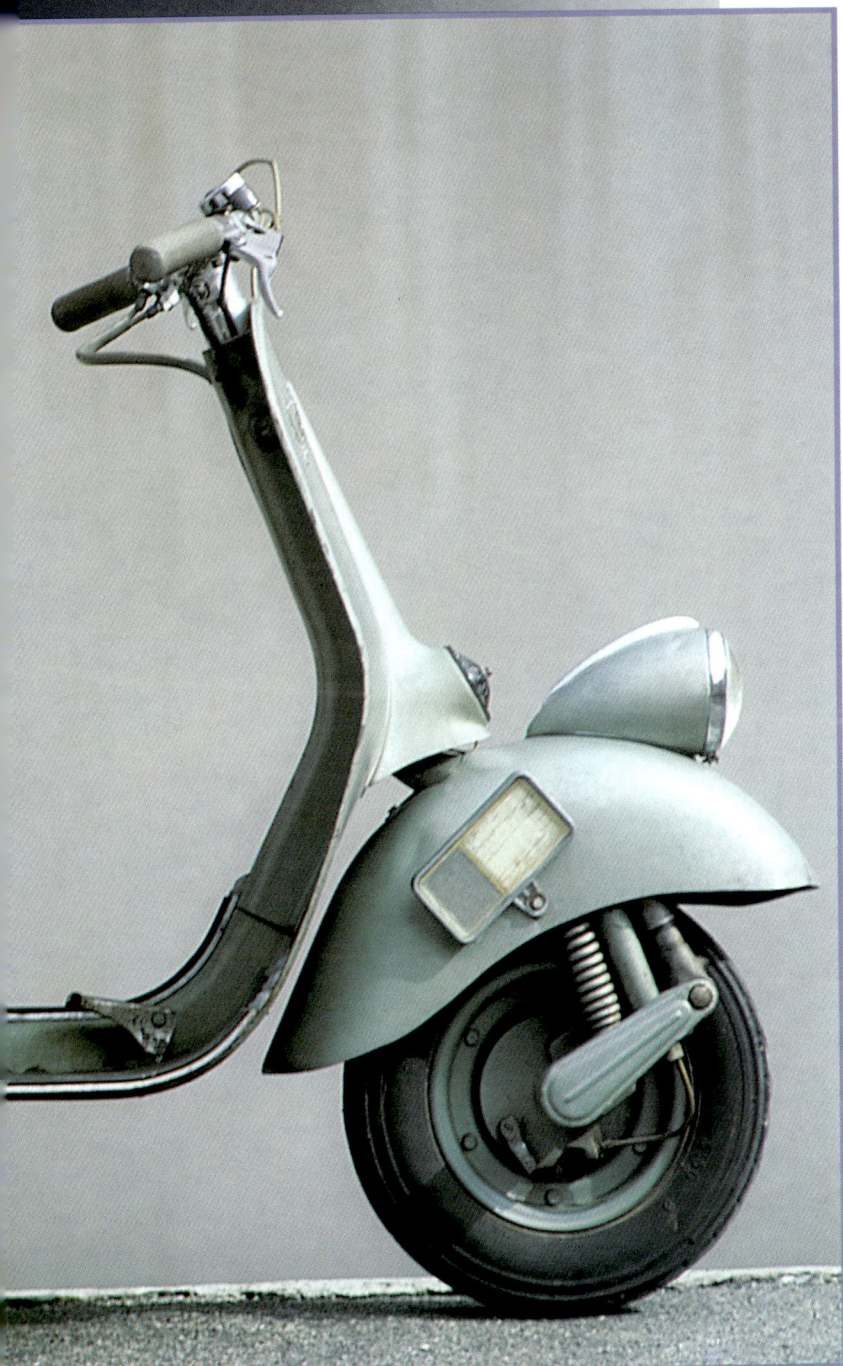

THE YEAR 1951 WAS ONE OF GREAT INNOVATIONS FOR THE VESPA: THE MOST IMPORTANT WAS THE ELIMINATION OF THE "RODS" OF THE GEAR SHIFT CONTROLS, REPLACED NOW BY FLEXIBLE CABLES. REAR SUSPENSION WAS EQUIPPED WITH A TELESCOPIC SHOCK ABSORBER. OTHER CHANGES INVOLVED THE SEAT (WIDER), THE BRAKE PEDAL, THE REAR RUNNING LIGHT AND THE HEADLIGHT (LARGER AND MOVED BACKWARD), THE MUFFLER, AND THE ARM THAT SUPPORTED THE ENGINE. LASTLY, A LITTLE BIT OF CONSIDERATION FOR THE PASSENGER: THE RACK WAS EXTENDED BACKWARD A GOOD 10 CM. TO MAKE A MORE COMFORTABLE SEAT.

125
1951

PART II

THE MESSAGE

ADVERTISING IS THE SOUL OF THE VESPA

alla loro felicità
manca solo la

Vespa

S cooters had never been particularly popular, even though their history extended back to the turn of the century when they first appeared on the stage of motoring history, like little motorized skateboards before their time.

Even the more sophisticated and elaborate models of the Thirties, so hard to use due to their lack of reliability, failed to persuade the motorcycle and automobile-buying public, who tended to consider scooters as something akin to toys.

Enrico Piaggio, however, knew that his Vespa was something different. His engineering and marketing

ADVERTISING FOR THE VESPA INITIALLY EMPHASIZED AFFORDABILITY AND EASY PAYMENT PLANS. THEN IT BEGAN TO UNDERSCORE VARIOUS QUALITIES OF THE VESPA THROUGH CLEAR AND UNDERSTANDABLE MESSAGES (BELOW, RIGHT TO LEFT): A LITTLE ELEPHANT EXPLAINED THAT THE SCOOTER WAS STRONG AND STURDY; WHILE A GLOWING SUN EXPLAINED THAT THE SCOOTER WAS FUN AND HEALTHY. THE THIRD MESSAGE WAS MORE SOPHISTICATED: THE VESPA (WHICH IS INVISIBLE) IS INDICATED AS THE ONLY MISSING COMPONENT OF A YOUNG COUPLE'S HAPPINESS. LATER, WHEN KIDS BEGAN TO "TAKE POSSESSION" OF THEIR PARENTS' DREAM OF HAPPINESS, ALL THAT WAS REQUIRED WAS THE TELEGRAPHIC LANGUAGE OF THE FUNNIES. A SIMPLE "VRROOUM!" WAS ENOUGH TO EXPLAIN THE VESPA'S PERFORMANCE.

team knew it too, and they swore by the technological modernity of their new vehicle that had nothing to do with what had gone before. How could they bring the mass market round to their way of thinking, when people were so mistrustful of a new product?
Simple: by saying that it was a new kind of vehicle, in an equally new kind of language. This too was a brilliant hunch, especially if we consider that at the time the very idea of a marketing policy was practically science fiction. But the message was developed, it was received, loud and clear, and the Vespa became an enormous commercial success. Among the many expla-

nations that can help us to understand the reason why, one was unquestionably the association of the new product with its manufacturer, Enrico Piaggio. Piaggio was an unusual man, almost a snob in his rigorous, quasi-nineteenth-century approach to industry. He hated socializing and he only frequented a small and restricted circle of old close friends, thought this circle included some of the best-known celebrities of the period. He was thus perceived as a serious and reliable person, qualities that were transferred overnight, as if by osmosis, to the Vespa, boosting its popularity immensely. The other factor was the decision, mentioned above, to mar-

ket the Vespa through the Lancia distribution network. The salesmen for this Turin-based carmaker added their own image to that of the Vespa, a flavor of elegance and esthetic perfection rubbing off from the Lancia automobiles. And so it came to pass that the scooter, which was certainly a mass-market product, became associated in the popular imagination with a certain kind of class, an association that always seemed to elude the Lambretta. The public has always felt this way and even now the Vespa holds a certain upper-class status in the scooter market.

However you look at it, the Vespa is a "classic." If you bought a Lancia, you were buying a distinctive and distinguished product. If you were buying a Vespa, you were buying the same set of images. In order to encourage and publicize the use of Vespas, Piaggio soon took up another weapon, quite familiar nowadays to advertisers and publicists. Whenever possible, Piaggio would pair the Vespa with a celebrity, especially a movie star, requesting and purchasing, as is so common even, a "product endorsement."

In this way, Piaggio triggered a process of imitation

NOWADAYS ADVERTISING MASSIVELY AFFECTS THE DEVELOPMENT OF LANGUAGE AND SPEECH, CONSTANTLY COINING NEW TERMS AND PHRASES WHICH IN TIME ENTER INTO EVERYDAY USE. BUT THE PIAGGIO COMPANY WAS AHEAD OF THE CROWD WHEN, IN 1956, IT USED "VESPIZZATEVI!"— LITERALLY, 'VESPIFY YOURSELVES!'—AS A SLOGAN, AMONG THE MOST FAMOUS LINES DEVELOPED BY THE PONTEDERA FIRM, BUT REPLACED IN 1969 BY THE SEDUCTIVE "CHI VESPA MANGIA LE MELE," LITERALLY 'IF YOU VESPA, YOU WILL HAVE A BITE OF THE APPLE."

THE ETERNAL TRIANGLE:
"HIM, HER, AND THE VESPA,"
IS ANOTHER CONSTANT
FEATURE OF THE PIAGGIO
IMAGE. THE VESPA FOR
LOVERS ALSO ENGENDERED
AN ENDLESS SERIES OF
PICTURE POSTCARDS THAT
LOVERS AND SWEETHEARTS
WOULD SEND EACH OTHER
FROM ALL OVER ITALY, WITH
LOTS OF HUGS AND KISSES.

and emulation that fed, on the one hand, upon the considerable promotional thrust of fashion, and on the other hand made use of current events and the skyrocketing popularity of other Italian figures. And the Vespa took wing, and flew....

In comparison with the other scooters that appeared on the market in the Fifties (there was not a single motorcycle manufacturer that failed to plunge into the market), the mechanical engineering of the Vespa was unquestionably more advanced and boasted a general cutting-edge conception along with superior performance and features in terms of both comfort and handling.

The front shield protected driver and passenger from rain and mud. The complete enclosure of the engine made it possible to ride a Vespa, as D'Ascanio put it, "even in your Sunday best" (the only decent clothes that many Italians had in those years) without fear of staining or ruining them, since there was no oil spray or leaking gas.

It was also possible to add a windshield, making it much more convenient to use the scooter in winter as well. For this and many other reasons, the Vespa managed to solve the problem of getting around for people who needed to use it every day, especially to go to work.

The Vespa, then, was actually a little two-wheeled auto-

27

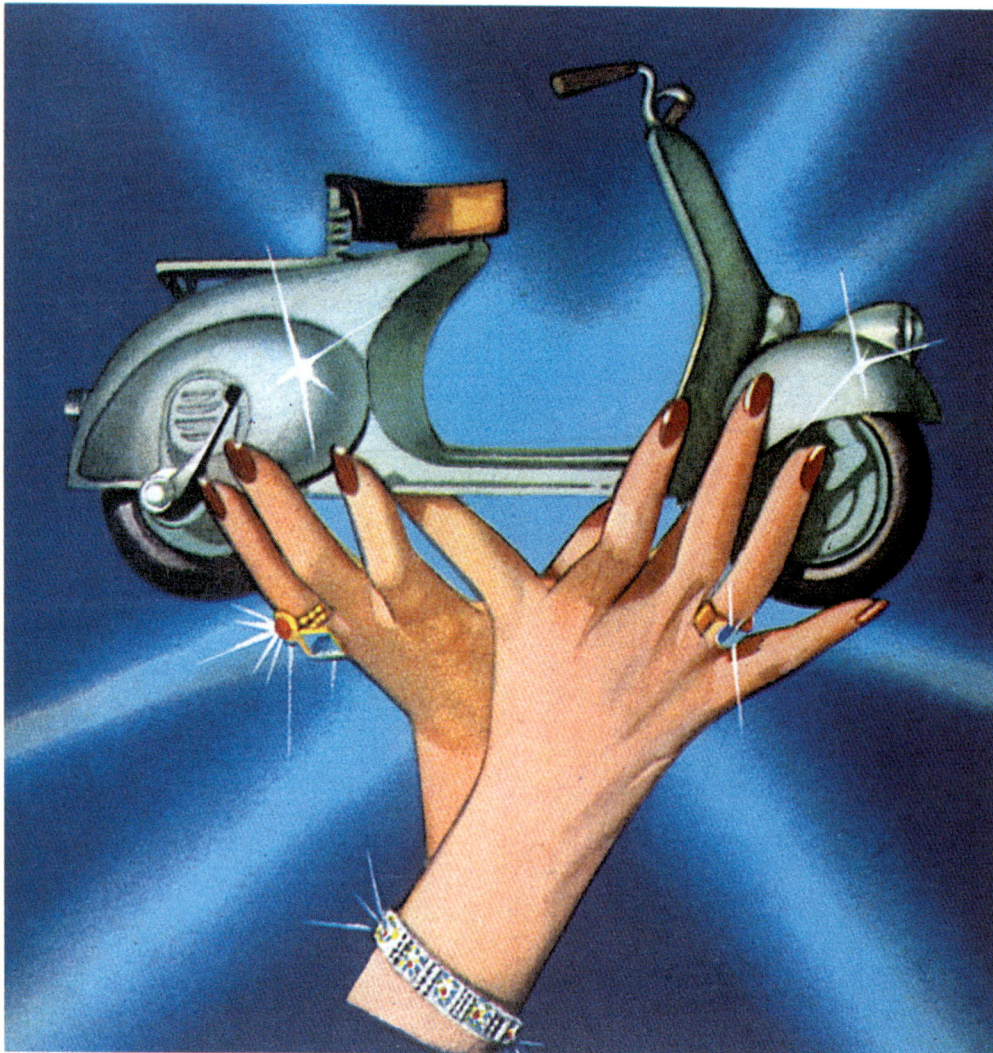

mobile, or perhaps we should say three-wheeled auto-mobile, since it carried a spare tire. In practical terms, however, it was as if it had four wheels, since it performed all the same functions as a runabout, often carrying entire families from one place to another.

It was therefore difficult to classify the Vespa as an ordinary scooter. Without a doubt it was, at once, a faithful working assistant, a way of having fun, and even a status symbol in an Italy that could envy even small luxuries…

Its reassuring image, in the meanwhile, contrasted ever more sharply with the more traditional image of the motorcycle. The classic two-wheeler was not enjoying any particular popularity, at least in those years, even though the first signals of a youth revolution were just arriving from the United States, nicely embodied by a young and reckless Marlon Brando straddling a powerful Triumph. The message of "The Wild One" was exciting but too dangerous, at least for now.

The Vespas that Audrey Hepburn and Gregory Peck rode in "Roman Holiday," on the other hand, were reassuring, refreshing, and eminently likable! In fact, many Piaggio advertising posters adopted this line, showing young and happy loving couples straddling their faithful Vespas.

THE VESPA, A CLASSY SCOOTER: A VERITABLE "GEM" THAT LOOKED EMINENTLY PRESENTABLE AMONG DIAMOND RINGS AND BRACELETS. THIS WAS ONE OF THE MANY MESSAGES THAT PIAGGIO PLACED IN THE PAGES OF MAGAZINES AROUND THE WORLD, IN THE WAKE OF A POPULARITY THAT SEEMED INEXHAUSTIBLE.

PIRELLI per lo scooter

DEPENDABILITY
UNSURPASSABLE
INDEPENDENCE

More and more people get ahead on a Vespa

The Vespa 125 c.c.   The Vespa 150 c.c.   The Vespa Gran Sport

Get ahead
see your Vespa dealer TODAY

il problema del posteggio

Aumentano gli automezzi
aumenta il traffico
aumentano gli ingorghi
i posteggi sono strapieni:

Cos'altro occorre per decidersi
a usare la Vespa?
Per la Vespa c'è sempre un posto.
Con la Vespa si risparmia
tempo, pazienza e denaro.

con la Vespa
non è un problema

THE "PRECIOUSNESS" OF THE VESPA TOOK ON AN INCREASING ARRAY OF CONNOTATIONS, AND WHEN PARKING BECAME SCARCE IN CROWDED CITIES EVERYWHERE: "WHAT COULD BE THE MOST PRECIOUS FEATURE OF A VESPA?" THE ANSWER WAS AUTOMATIC: "FOR A VESPA, THERE IS ALWAYS A PARKING PLACE. WITH A VESPA, YOU WILL SAVE TIME, MONEY, AND ESPECIALLY, YOUR NERVES..."

In order to consolidate the felicitous image that had thus been constructed, on 9 October 1949 the Piaggio company organized a visit to the pope, Pius XII, and made an official papal gift of a Vespa. The Holy Father, according to the newspapers of the time, pronounced a benediction over the Vespa and, after hearing about its many features, bestowed it upon a missionary father just leaving for the Far East, thus transforming the Papal Vespa into an evangelistic tool!

A remarkable role, but not unprecedented. In fact, like Pirandello's "characters in search of an author," the Vespa was constantly fitting into new roles. Besides wearing the missionary's habit, the Vespa donned every imaginable outfit and garb: camouflage uniforms (it fought with distinction in Algeria and even in Vietnam...), the khaki outfits of African explorers, the tattered clothing of great world travellers...

The Vespa, in short, took every opportunity to show off its flexibility. In fact, the directors of SARPI, and especially the engineer Barnato and Renzo Tassinari worked tirelessly on every front, seeking to take advantage of every occasion, including negative ones.

For instance, the Russians, scorning "capitalist" patents and trademarks, and well protected by their Iron Curtain, copied the Vespa detail by detail and manufactured it for use in their home market, as a "glorious Soviet invention." The Piaggio launched its gentlemanly and cunning response in newspaper advertisements: "The Russians use the Sputnik to travel in space, but to travel on the ground they rely on Vespas..."

The Pontedera firm was present, over the years, at all the most important trade fairs and auto shows, but where the marketing arm of Piaggio really outdid itself was at the Fiera Campionaria di Milano, Milan's immense trade fair.

In particular, during the first few years of Vespa production, the Fiera Campionaria was always used as a stage upon which to amaze and impress the public with especially innovative installations and presentations, unfailingly winning great notice in the press, trade and general alike.

In 1948 the "Sciame d'Argento," or "Silver Swarm," was organized, a meet and rally that drew 2,000 "vespisti" to Milan, assembling at the inauguration of that season's Fiera Campionaria, astonishing those visiting the fair. In 1949 the Piaggio stand was the most popular one in the Milan fair: this time the company had reproduced the entire Vespa assembly line. The public could watch in astonishment as Vespa after Vespa was manufactured before their eyes.

In 1950 Piaggio won space on the front pages of newspapers throughout Italy by bringing an enormous "Vespone" to Milan, more than three meters tall.

Without a doubt, these were spectacular undertakings, designed to generate discussion of the Vespa, not only for its unquestionable technical and practical merits, but also to give it a general identity as a product always at the cutting edge and... in fashion.

All of this of course was eminently evident in the comments about the Vespa that appeared in both the Italian and international press.

The "Neue Wiener Tageszeitung" published, for instance, on 27 April 1950, a report from Italy under this indicative headline: "Rome, Capital of the Vespa," while the "Frankfurter Rudschum", a few days later, observed that it was "by now impossible to imagine the streets of Italy without those quick and lively little vehicles."

In the Italian press, articles appeared reporting more distinctive and curious episodes, which nonetheless tended to reinforce the image of the Vespa.

In February 1951 "Il Messaggero" presented the Vespa as a paladin of justice, as well as being... faster than a Lambretta: "A daring chase involving two motorscooters took place yesterday at Centocelle," the newspaper reported in its local news section.

"Two young men, Pasquale Di Somma, 17, and Mario Vitali, 20, saw a Lambretta on the street, they hopped onto it, and zoomed off.

The owner Eugenio Nicolini, immediately realized his scooter had been stolen and summoned two carabinieri, or paramilitary policemen, sergeant Alberto Del

HOW MANY MOVIES HAVE FEATURED VESPAS? WE COULD PROBABLY LIST HUNDREDS. THE MOST FAMOUS, OF COURSE, WAS "ROMAN HOLDIDAY" (1953) WITH GREGORY PECK AND AUDREY HEPBURN. BUT THERE WAS NOT AN ACTOR OR ACTRESS OF THE FIFTIES AND SIXTIES WHO DIDN'T RIDE A VESPA AT LEAST ONCE. AMONG OTHERS, WE SHOULD MENTION MARCELLO MASTROIANNI, LUCIA BOSÉ, WILLIAM HOLDEN, MARISA ALLASIO, AND VITTORI GASSMANN (IN THE PHOTOGRAPHS).

Vecchio and deputy sergeant Adone Stefanini. The two policemen jumped onto their Vespa and took off after the stolen Lambretta. After a half-hour chase, they caught up with the thieves at Prenestino."

The Vespa had become such a vehicle of social change in the Fifties that it played starring role in films and books. In 1950, the German production house Jungen Film Union made a musical ("Der Doctor Nachifalter") that featured, for the first time on the silver screen, twenty Vespas.

Obviously, Piaggio promoted the image of its motorscooter through particularly popular advertising campaigns as well.

Ever since the Vespa 98 appeared on the market, in fact, it was decided to accompany the scooter with an adequate advertising message, supplying the public with information, encouragement to buy, and a constant presence in the leading publications, whether specialized or not.

At first, Piaggio had supplied chiefly "technical" information to the consumer public, along with indications of the price, details regarding the warranty, the service network, and the industrial growth and progress of the company itself.

Then Piaggio decided to change its approach, and the advertising began to burgeon with lovely women and cheerful sophisticated slogans.

One of these slogans, the most famous, was based on the Italian imperative: "Vespizzatevi," literally, 'Vespify Yourselves.' The first poster with this message appeared in 1956, and it is interesting to note that the Vespa was considered both a vehicle for fun and for work, useful even in farming.

Advertising for the Vespa, in the meanwhile, naturally continued to emphasize the technical features of the vehicle: the efficiency of the controls grouped on the handlebars, the small wheels, easy access to the engine, the small but functional luggage rack, and the ease with which a flat tire could be changed (not a remote likelihood at the time, considering the general conditions of Italian roads).

This advertising drive was so effective that Vespas almost immediately became products so overloaded with meanings and connotations that in time the Vespa itself became a medium with which to advertise other products.

Finally, an indication of the Vespa's newfound status: in April of 1953 the first Italian television broadcast took place, during the 30th Fiera Campionaria di Milano, and on the stage, along with many other stars of stage and screen, clearly invited to attract interest in the new medium, was one diva among many... a brand-new Vespa. If there was any need of an official coronation as a pop cult icon, here it was!

TRAVELLING BY VESPA IS A FORM OF INTENSE HAPPINESS. WHERE THERE'S A VESPA, THERE'S A PARTY. THE VESPA IS A WAY TO PARADISE. VESPAS WORK.... MIRACLES! "IN FACT," ACCORDING TO ONE SLOGAN FROM THE SIXTIES, "THE VESPA SHORTENS YOUR WORKING HOURS AND LENGTHENS YOUR LEISURE TIME." AFTER THAT AMAZING LIST OF SELF-ATTRIBUTED COMPLIMENTS, WE CAN UNDERSTAND THE GLOWING SMILE OF THE ACTRESS ANGIE DICKINSON. BUT WE CAN'T BE SURE IF THE CHILD AND THE WOMAN RUNNING AFTER HER WANT HER AUTOGRAPH OR THE VESPA'S...

THE VESPA GS (GRAN SPORT), IMMEDIATELY GIVEN THE AFFECTIONATE NICKNAME OF "VESPONE," OR 'BIG WASP,' WAS THE SPECTACULAR NEW DEVELOPMENT PRESENTED BY THE PONTEDERA FIRM IN THE NOVEMBER OF 1954. BECAUSE OF ITS SPORTY FEATURES, IT IMMEDIATELY BECAME ONE OF THE MOST POPULAR MODELS. ITS AGGRESSIVE STYLING WAS MUCH ADMIRED; ITS 150 CC. ENGINE WAS QUITE IMPRESSIVE; THE FOUR-SPEED TRANSMISSION WAS UNIVERSALLY PRAISED. IT ALSO FEATURED A NEW, TWO-PERSON SEAT, AND WAS THE FIRST VESPA TO FEATURE 10-INCH WHEELS. MOST IMPORTANTLY, IT COULD ATTAIN THE NOTABLE SPEED OF 100 KILOMETERS PER HOUR.

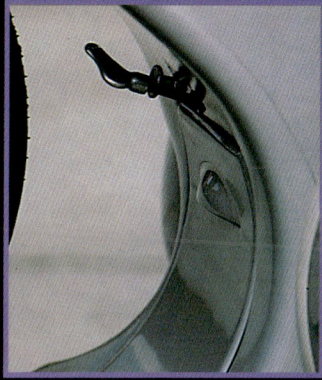

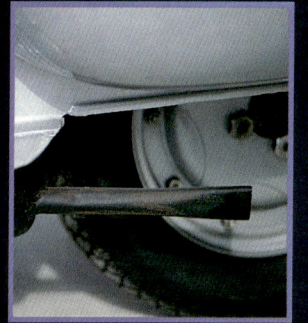

Engine: horizontal two-stroke single-cylinder; 145.45 cc. displacement, 8 hp at 7,500 rpm, Dell'Orto UB23 carburetor, four-speed gearbox, lubrication with 5 percent mixture, top speed 100 kph.

150
ACMA
MILITARE

THE VESPA HAS ALSO PERFORMED MILITARY SERVICE, WITH THE CAMOUFLAGE MARKINGS OF MANY DIFFERENT ARMIES. IT SAW COMBAT IN ALGERIA, SOUTH AMERICA, AND EVEN VIETNAM... IN 1952, THE FRENCH BRANCH OF PIAGGIO, ACMA, DEVELOPED A SPECIAL VERSION FOR THE FRENCH ARMY, WHICH COULD EVEN MOUNT A SMALL CANNON OR A BAZOOKA, WITH AMMUNITION... IF NECESSARY, THIS VEHICLE COULD BE DROPPED BY PARACHUTE. IN THIS CASE, THE "COMBAT" VESPA HAD A TUBULAR CASE THAT PROTECTED IT FROM IMPACT WITH THE GROUND.

Engine: horizontal two-stroke single-cylinder, 145.45 cc. displacement, 4.5 hp at 4,500 rpm, Solex 17 B carburetor, three-speed gearbox, lubrication with 5 percent mixture, top speed 65 kph.

SOCIETY

BETTER TO LIVE ONE DAY AS A VESPA…

*T*he Vespa was, right from the beginning, a "concrete" product. Its features (cutting edge technological performance, handy use, and handsome design) alone added up to explosive "mixture." To count on a positive and immediate popularity on the market might have therefore seemed like an obvious approach. But things were not that simple. A considerable portion of the Vespa's success was the result of a series of unusually fresh and innovative marketing decisions that managed to create an aura of cheerful likeability around this innovative vehicle.

This happened, however, only after the initial advertising strategy was abandoned. The very first commercial launch of the Vespa, in fact, involved nothing more than informing the public about the scooter's performance, variations in its price, and conditions of payment.

At the beginning of the Fifties, however, the promotional philosophy for the Vespa, or perhaps we should say, the Vespa image, changed entirely. The advertising became more glamorous and aggressive. It made use of more sophisticated tools of communication. It relied on forms of

IN 1951, THE PIAGGIO COMPANY PUBLISHED THEIR FIRST CALENDAR, WITH ILLUSTRATIONS BY FRANCO MOSCA. ON THE FOLLOWING PAGES A NUMBER OF PAGES APPEAR FROM THOSE CALENDARS, SHOWING GLOBE-TROTTING WOMEN. AS IF TO SAY, THANKS TO THE VESPA, EVERYONE CAN DISCOVER NEW HORIZONS.

Mars

D	L	M	M	J	V	S
				1	2	3
4	5	6	7	8	9	10
11	12	13	14	15	16	17
18	19	20	21	22	23	24
25	26	27	28	29	30	31

Avril

D	L	M	M	J	V	S
1	2	3	4	5	6	7
8	9	10	11	12	13	14
15	16	17	18	19	20	21
22	23	24	25	26	27	28
29	30					

1951

Mai | *Juin* | *1951*

D	L	M	M	J	V	S
	1	2	3	4	5	
6	7	8	9	10	11	12
13	14	15	16	17	18	19
20	21	22	23	24	25	26
27	28	29	30	31		

D	L	M	M	J	V	S
					1	2
3	4	5	6	7	8	9
10	11	12	13	14	15	16
17	18	19	20	21	22	23
24	25	26	27	28	29	30

Septembre | *Octobre* | *1951*

D	L	M	M	J	V	S
						1
2	3	4	5	6	7	8
9	10	11	12	13	14	15
16	17	18	19	20	21	22
23/30	24	25	26	27	28	29

D	L	M	M	J	V	S
	1	2	3	4	5	6
7	8	9	10	11	12	13
14	15	16	17	18	19	20
21	22	23	24	25	26	27
28	29	30	31			

Juillet | *Août* | *1951*

D	L	M	M	J	V	S
1	2	3	4	5	6	7
8	9	10	11	12	13	14
15	16	17	18	19	20	21
22	23	24	25	26	27	28
29	30	31				

D	L	M	M	J	V	S
			1	2	3	4
5	6	7	8	9	10	11
12	13	14	15	16	17	18
19	20	21	22	23	24	25
26	27	28	29	30	31	

TOURISM AND THE VESPA: THE COMBINATION IS A CONSTANT IN THE CALENDARS BY FRANCO MOSCA. WITH A VESPA, YOU CAN REACH ANY DESTINATION, SEEMS TO BE THE MESSAGE CONVEYED BY THE GIRLS THAT APPEAR ON THESE PAGES. THIS ADVERTISING STRATEGY FOUND ITS CONFIRMATION IN THE HUNDREDS OF VESPA CLUBS THAT BEGAN TO FORM IN ITALY AND ACROSS EUROPE.

manipulation that had yet to be extensively exploited.

The first, and perhaps the most spectacular, example of this change of direction was the calendar that Piaggio began to publish in 1951. These calendars immediately became enormously popular and became even more so over the years. A great deal of words have been spoken and written about the "phenomenon" of the Piaggio calendar, which not only documented the development of various models of Vespa but also served as a precious mirror of the times and fashions that emerged over the years.

To judge the phenomenon as merely frivolous, however, simply because the calendars featured a bevy of lovely girls, would be a serious error. Their style and activities in fact constitutes a precious and complete historical document, in which an entire generation can still recognize its own past. All these girls together expressed the desire of an entire nation to leave the past—and the world war—behind it, and seek out new and more encouraging frontiers.

This anthology of paper pinups was distinguished, in fact, by its unconscious participation in the world around it that was constantly changing and evolving, and thus—willy nilly—becoming itself a document of lifestyle and fashion. The Piaggio calendars recorded, year after year, the incessant phases of esthetic progress and the refinement of the tastes of the consumer public; changes that on the one hand were seen in the evolution of an industrial product like the Vespa, and on the other in the transformation of the type of increasingly modern, increasingly independent, and—considering the times—increasingly liberated women portrayed.

Various factors and trends contributed to the creation of the Piaggio calendars. The first ones featured illustrations (with a style typical of movie posters) emphasizing particularly seductive women.

One factor in this decision was certainly the popularity at the time of color periodicals ("Grand Hotel," "La Domenica del Corriere") which tended to use brightly colored drawings, while the photography was only black and white. The influence of these periodicals was clearly decisive. The overall style was also influenced by the enormous popularity in Italy of romance novels and beauty pageants.

A picturesque part of that world, however superficial and playful, thus entered the Piaggio calendars that in those years, more than in the present day, became a fundamental item in the furnishings of home, offices, and stores, representing an important form of entertainment and escape: dreams and hopes of a life seen through rose-colored glasses. Lots of different girls, we have already said, so many different

types, so many different faces, but in the final analysis, all one character, all one personality: the Vespa girl, a lively young lady who, through her loveliness (but also through her likeable personality), attracts the attention of an infinite array of people belonging to every walk of life. There was, however, more to the Vespa girl than that.

First of all, she interpreted the spirit of the Vespa. From the very first calendar, in 1951, the girls depicted were all irrepressible globe-trotters. They were shown as tourists travelling around the world: we see them in the shadow of the Sphinx, touching up their makeup in front of Nôtre Dame, enjoying the local folklore in Holland.

But they were also very athletic: in the 1952 calendar, for example, they are shown skiing, swimming, and of course wearing skimpy bikinis. Naturally, they are shown on golf courses and riding horseback with great skill. All of this without ever abandoning their Vespas, their constant and loyal companion in every adventure. That is not all: they go sailing, they attend road races, they work as stewardesses, and they pitch tent and go camping. Active though they may have been, they certainly did not neglect the intellectual side of life: they listened to good music and they were often seen in artist's studios. They loved animals and among their favorite dogs we note that they have at least one exceedingly elegant tawny Afghan hound, showing that they were also trendsetters: the Afghan was a trend that did not explode until the Sixties. We could say many other things about the girls that emerged from the pen of Franco Mosca, who drew the scenes that appeared in the calendars from 1951 to 1954 (a drawing for every two months). How many men (young and old) fell in love with them? How many wallpapered their bedrooms with those images, perhaps slightly unreal, but surely seductive and appealing? And then, suddenly, one New Year's Eve, they disappeared and were replaced by the first photographs of models, real girls in flesh and blood, lovely, alluring, femmes fatales, and of course, even easier to dream about and fall in love with. The Vespa, too, had become more lovely, increasingly streamlined and elegant, more and more of a diva. Thanks to its new design, it looked pretty good alongside the equally perfect bodies of its equally well-designed partners.

giugno

D		3	10	17	24
L		4	11	18	25
M		5	12	19	26
M		6	13	20	27
G		7	14	21	28
V	1	8	15	22	29
S	2	9	16	23	30

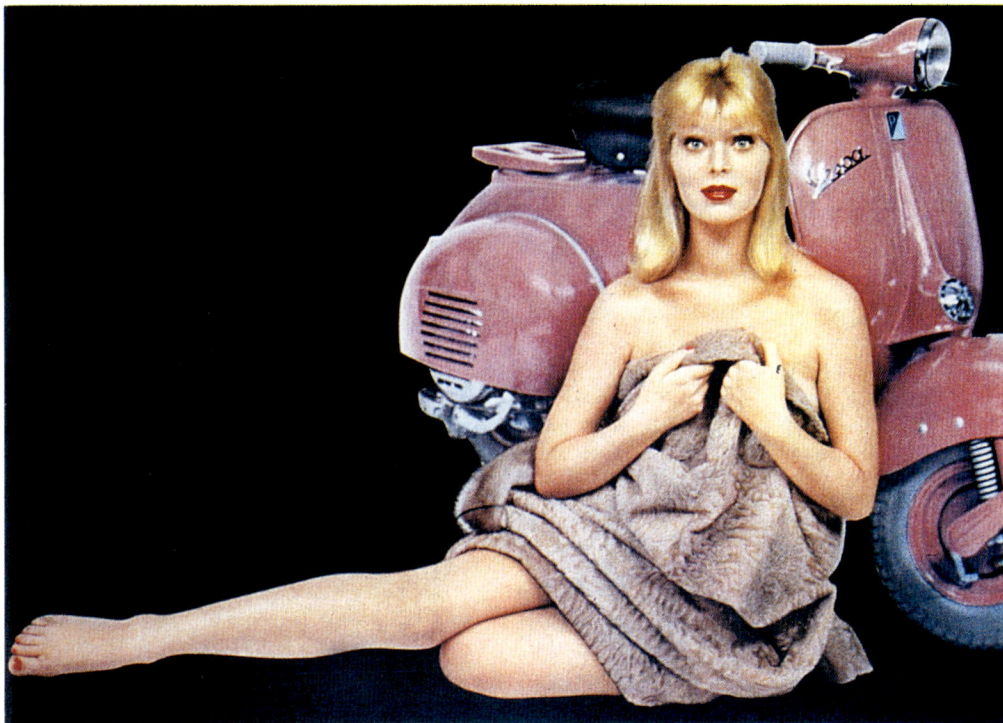

IN 1959 THE PIAGGIO CALENDAR FEATURED AN UNUSUAL BLACK BACKGROUND TO EMPHASIZE THE RICH ARRAY OF PASTELS THAT DISTINGUISHED THE NEW MODELS OF VESPA

ON THE RIGHT AND ON THE FACING PAGE, A SERIES OF PAGES FROM THE 1956 CALENDAR, WHICH FEATURED PHOTOGRAPHS INSTEAD OF THE MORE TRADITIONAL ILLUSTRATIONS. THE NEW IDEA, INTRODUCED THE YEAR PREVIOUS, WAS VERY POPULAR. IN FACT, IN THE SECOND YEAR THE DECISION WAS MADE TO HOLD A BEAUTY CONTEST TO ESTABLISH WHICH OF THE TWELVE GIRLS PORTRAYED WAS JUDGED THE PRETTIEST. BY POPULAR ACCLAIM, THE TITLE WENT TO MISS JUNE.

The duos were increasingly competitive: who was the fairest of them all?

In 1956, in order to determine just who was the fairest of them all, a write-in contest was announced to elect the calendar-miss of the year; it was possible to vote by mailing in Piaggio coupons that were published in the four most popular Italian weekly magazines. That year, the winner was Miss June, and in later years, the winners were generally girls published in summer months: possibly something to do with their attire...

In any case, in part due to the beauty contest, this marked the beginning of the most successful period of the Piaggio calendar which, in 1959, was run on a black background to emphasize the new pastel hues of the Vespa. In 1960 (one of the most successful and collectible calendar years) the Piaggio calendar became an important "testimonial" of the Pontedera firm and an advertising tool of unparalleled effectiveness. To mention a few numbers, in 1965 there were 257,000 copies of the calendar in three editions and eight languages as well as 900,000 copies of a pocket version, to satisfy the frantic demands that were pouring into the offices in Genoa from all over the world: that year, 10,000 letters arrived from Indonesia alone. In the wake of this popularity the most beautiful, most famous and even the most artistically committed actresses all clamored to appear in the calendar. Among the stars who attended this Vespa-party we should mention Elsa Martinelli, Sylva Koscina, Rossana Podestà, Catherine Spaak, Paola Pitagora, Stefania Sandrelli, the Kessler twins...

julio

D	L	M	M	J	V	S
	1	2	3	4	5	6
7	8	9	10	11	12	13
14	15	16	17	18	19	20
21	22	23	24	25	26	27
28	29	30	31			

abril

D	L	M	M	J	V	S
	1	2	3	4	5	6
7	8	9	10	11	12	13
14	15	16	17	18	19	20
21	22	23	24	25	26	27
28	29	30				

marzo

D	L	M	M	J	V	S
					1	2
3	4	5	6	7	8	9
10	11	12	13	14	15	16
17	18	19	20	21	22	23
24/31	25	26	27	28	29	30

junio

D	L	M	M	J	V	S
						1
2	3	4	5	6	7	8
9	10	11	12	13	14	15
16	17	18	19	20	21	22
23/30	24	25	26	27	28	29

Things changed at the end of the Sixties when the economic boom began to show its dark side. The girls of the Piaggio calendar suddenly rediscovered nature, in a bellwether of environmental concerns that the Vespa as well, timely as ever, would begin to emphasize, touting itself as the cleanest means of transportation in the city. The 1968 calendar, in fact, offered a mix of seaside and scooters, a feminine image that was entirely different from the ones that had gone before. No longer dolls and tomatoes, no more movie stars and divas—instead, ordinary women.

No longer posing for the camera, but simply relaxing, thinking, enjoying themselves, living their lives in a joyful and natural landscape. And so we see a new woman, more mature than in the past, more realistic and less stereotypical, natural and simple. Exactly like the Vespa of more recent years.

PIN-UPS

FROM THE SIXTIES ONWARDS, THE PIAGGIO CALENDAR BEGAN TO DISPLAY MORE COLOR AND MORE... SEDUCTION. THE GIRLS WERE EVER MORE SKIMPILY CLAD: MISS JANUARY, FOR INSTANCE, WAS PHOTOGRAPHED NUDE TAKING A BATH IN A TUB NEAR A PLATE OF FRUIT (OUT OF SEASON, OF COURSE). WHAT IS THE MEANING OF THIS COMBINATION? PERHAPS SOMEONE WAS ALREADY THINKING OF THE FORERUNNER TO THE MOST FAMOUS OF THE PIAGGIO COMPANY'S SLOGANS: "CHI VESPA MANGIA LE MELE..." LITERALLY 'IF YOU VESPA, YOU WILL HAVE A BITE OF THE APPLE..." IN EFFECT, THE LIKEABLE LITTLE SCOOTER BUILT BY THE PONTEDERA FIRM, WAS UNDERGOING A SIGNIFICANT METAMORPHOSIS: MOTHER AND FATHER NOW OWNED AN AUTOMOBILE, AND THE VESPA WAS GETTING READY TO BECOME THE "FORBIDDEN FRUIT" OF A NEW AND YOUNGER GENERATION.

1960: All of Italy was going crazy over television. John F. Kennedy was sworn in as president of the United States. Livio Berruti took a gold medal at the Olympics. The first commercial jets flew from Rome to Milan. The Vespa finally complied with the Italian traffic laws.

DICEMBRE

D	L	M	M	G	V	S
				1	2	3
4	5	6	7	8	9	10
11	12	13	14	15	16	17
18	19	20	21	22	23	24
25	26	27	28	29	30	31

SMILES

THE 1961 PIAGGIO CALENDAR REPEATED WHAT HAD BEEN DONE THE PREVIOUS YEAR: THE PHOTOGRAPHS WERE STUDIO SHOTS, AS WAS FASHIONABLE AT THE TIME, WITH SPECIAL PROPS AND SETTINGS TO MAKE THE MODELS SEEM RELAXED AND NATURAL. AT FIRST GLANCE, THE PHOTOGRAPHS SHOW NO PARTICULAR COMMUNICATIONS STRATEGY: IT SEEMS LIKE ALL THAT IS BEING DONE IS PAIRING THE VESPA WITH A NUMBER OF SMILING BEAUTY QUEENS. BUT THOSE SEDUCTIVE GAZES CONCEAL A SUBTLE MESSAGE. THEY SEEM TO BE CREATING A SENSE OF COMPLICITY BETWEEN CUSTOMER AND THE VESTA, IN AN IMAGINARY TRIANGLE THAT MAKES IT THE FUNDAMENTAL VEHICLE FOR AN AMOROUS CONQUEST.

1961: Yuri Gagarin was the first man in space. Fiat introduced the new 1300/1500 models. Construction continued on Italy's main highway, the Autostrada del Sole. More than 1.5 million Vespas manufactured since 1946.

GIUGNO

D	L	M	M	G	V	S
				1	2	3
4	5	6	7	8	9	10
11	12	13	14	15	16	17
18	19	20	21	22	23	24
25	26	27	28	29	30	

DICEMBRE

NOVEMBRE

OTTOBRE

MAGGIO

LUGLIO

AGOSTO

SETTEMBRE

DIVAS

In 1962 the Piaggio calendar featured the debut of the faces (and bodies) of the most famous film stars of the moment. This change in direction was determined by the international nature of the Vespa, perhaps the best known (and most widespread) product of Italian industry in the world. And so it became necessary to create a more modern and less provincial image. Ahead of its time, Piaggio therefore invented 12 product endorsements at a single stroke. The charm of the Vespa went hand-in-hand with the charm of Mylène Demongeot, Sylva Koscina, Rossana Podestà... The settings were varied and there was little reference to the seasons depicted.

1962: The blonde and lovely Marilyn Monroe was found dead of an overdose of sleeping pills. Italian fashion invented ready-to-wear. Piaggio introduced the GS 160: new frame, new Vespa styling.

Mylène Demongeot

JUNI

S	M	D	M	D	F	S
					1	2
3	4	5	6	7	8	9
10	11	12	13	14	15	16
17	18	19	20	21	22	23
24	25	26	27	28	29	30

DEZEMBER

NOVEMBER

OKTOBER

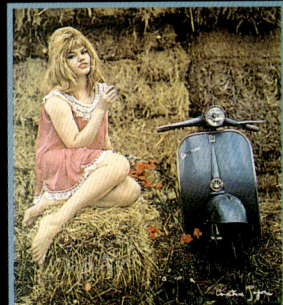

MAI

JULI

AUGUST

SEPTEMBER

TOP MODELS

THE STRATEGY OF USING LOVELY WOMEN REMAINED UNCHANGED IN 1963 WHEN THE CALENDAR OF MOVIE STARS WAS REPEATED IDENTICALLY. THE SUCCESS AND POPULARITY OF THE PREVIOUS YEAR'S CALENDAR FORCED THE EXECUTIVES OF PIAGGIO TO TAKE THIS LINE, LIMITING THE CHANGES TO A SELECTION OF NEW FACES TO GO WITH THE NEW MODEL VESPAS. MAKING THEIR DEBUTS WERE THE LOVELY CAROL BAKER, THE FRESH CATHERINE SPAAK, THE FASCINATING GLORIA PAUL, AND THE ABUNDANT JAYNE MANSFIELD. THEIR RELATIONSHIP WITH THE VARIOUS VESPAS FOUND A CREDIBLE JUSTIFICATION IN THE POPULARITY THAT BOTH THEY AND THE LITTLE SCOOTERS ENJOYED AMONG THE GENERAL PUBLIC.

1963: Pope John XXIII, John The Good, died. He was succeeded by Pope Paul VI. Jim Clark won the world Formula 1 championship. Brigitte Bardot launched the "two piece" bathing suit. The 150 GL was introduced, one of the loveliest Vespas ever built.

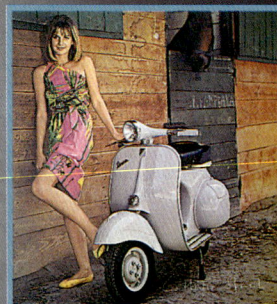

OTTOBRE

D	L	M	M	G	V	S
		1	2	3	4	5
6	7	8	9	10	11	12
13	14	15	16	17	18	19
20	21	22	23	24	25	26
27	28	29	30	31		

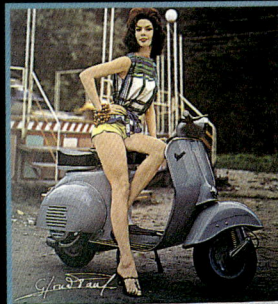

DICEMBRE

NOVEMBRE

SETTEMBRE

MAGGIO

GIUGNO

LUGLIO

AGOSTO

SEXY

IN 1964, THE PIAGGIO CALEN-
DAR WAS SUDDENLY FACED
WITH A DAUNTING RIVAL: THE
PIRELLI CALENDAR. BUT THESE WERE TWO
VERY DIFFERENT CREATURES. THE
MONTHS OF PIAGGIO'S VESPA CALENDAR
WERE STILL ILLUSTRATED BY FAMOUS
ACTRESSES, SOME OF THEM QUITE
SEXY (LIKE A PNEUMATIC SANDRA
MILO FOR THE MONTH OF JULY,
PEEPING OUT FROM BEHIND THE
FRONT SHIELD OF A VESPA 150,
OR A PROVOCATIVE SCILLA GABEL
FOR THE MONTH OF SEPTEMBER).
THE PIRELLI CALENDAR, ON THE
OTHER HAND, TOOK THE NEW AND SOPHIS-
TICATED PATH OF REVEALING ALL SORTS
OF ANATOMICAL DETAILS. THE PIAGGIO
MESSAGE WAS MUCH MORE TRADITIONAL.
THE ONLY NEW DEVELOPMENT: FACES
BORROWED FROM THE POPULAR NEW
MEDIUM OF TELEVISION, SUCH AS THE
KESSLER TWINS, IN JUNE.

1964: Beatles mania hits Italy. Mary Quant invents the mini-skirt in London, while at Pontedera Piaggio creates the Vespa 50, the scooter for the fourteen-year-olds.

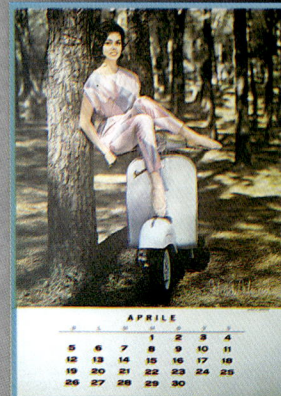

SCILLA GABEL

SETTEMBRE

D	L	M	M	G	V	S
		1	2	3	4	5
6	7	8	9	10	11	12
13	14	15	16	17	18	19
20	21	22	23	24	25	26
27	28	29	30			

DICEMBRE

NOVEMBRE

OTTOBRE

MAGGIO

GIUGNO

LUGLIO

AGOSTO

PART IV

THE PEOPLE

THE VESPA AND ALL ITS LITTLE VESPAS

T he idea of bringing together in some way all of the Vespa owners, and transforming this communion of vehicles into a general communion of people was yet another of the factors that did so much to promote the popularity of the young Piaggio scooter.

The idea occurred to Renzo Tassinari, a former editor of the sports daily, "Gazzetta dello Sport," and later, editor of the competing periodical, "Corriere dello Sport." After the war, Tassinari went to work for Piaggio at Pontedera. It was his job to organize the Vespa presence at the Fiera di Milano, or Milan trade fair, in 1948. Tassinari invented for the occasion the "Sciama d'Argento," or 'silver swarm,' which was an assembly of 2,000 Vespa riders who congregated, en

A "VESPISTA" TRAVELING ALONE JUST ZIPS DOWN THE ROAD. A GROUP OF "VESPISTI" DON'T ZIP, THEY "SWARM." AFTER THE FIRST SPECTACULAR MEET IN MILAN IN 1948, OWNERS OF VESPA SCOOTERS BEGAN TO FORM CLUBS WHICH EVENTUALLY BLOOMED INTO THE NETWORK OF VESPA CLUBS OF ITALY. THEY QUICKLY BEGAN TO ORGANIZE MEETS, RALLIES, TOURS, AND OTHER EVENTS. BELOW, A PHOTOGRAPH OF THE PARTICIPANTS IN THE FIRST SAN GIUSTO MEET. THE "VESPISTI" (AND AS YOU CAN SEE, THE OCCASIONAL CLANDESTINE "LAMBRETTISTA") RIDE DOWN THE STREETS OF TRIESTE, LED BY THE PRESIDENT OF THE LOCAL VESPA CLUB, SIGNOR FERIGO.

VESPA CLUB ITALIA
CAMPIONATO VESPISTICO ITALIANO 1960
LIVORNO - PESCARA - 10 LUGLIO 1960

masse, in Milan, the capital of Lombardy.

When the Vespas actually all arrived, people remained open-mouthed and newspapers and magazines made a seven-day wonder of the event. That marked the beginning of an unprecedented social phenomenon that grew to encompass international dimensions; though in the short term, on a more pragmatic level, it served primarily to encourage the sales and use of Vespas.

"Swarming" through the streets and roads of Italy, touring the country's monuments, discovering new and unfamiliar landscapes, and above all, meeting so many new people after years of wartime diffidence and solitude, was for many Italians a jolt of pure adrenalin. The idea of the "swarm" was a popular one, indeed it immediately galvanized a mass reaction. Following the example of Milan, anyone who had a Vespa sought out someone else with a Vespa. And as a result, the first clubs began to form. All of those clubs, in turn, one after another, began to amalgamate into the Vespa Clubs that the agents of SARPI had established in the meanwhile.

At first their activities were limited to organizing outings along easy, short routes. Later, larger assemblies and meets were attempted. Finally, mass "excursions" outside the Italian borders were undertaken.

The first, and perhaps the most important of these events was the so-called "raid" entitled "In Svizzera a Volo di Vespa," or 'Fly Your Vespa to Switzerland,' which the tire-

less Tassinari organized in March 1949: a 750 km. trip, departing from Como, at an average speed of 45 kph. There were 73 Vespa riders (including 8 women). This was of course much more than a bunch of friends on an outing; it was a full-fledged marketing campaign. Suffice it to point out that the column was accompanied by the entire top management of Piaggio, heading the procession. Even D'Ascanio was there, at the front of the line. He knew that right at that moment his Vespa was setting out to conquer Europe.

The next step occurred the following year, on 23 October, when the presidents of all the Vespa Clubs of Italy—31 in number—assembled at the Hotel Belmare in Viareggio for the First National Conference of the Vespa Clubs of Italy. On that day, coordinating and supervisory was established for all the Vespa Clubs. At the same meeting, a statute was approved and the national symbol was chosen.

The stated goal of the Vespa Clubs was: "To promote, support, and defend the interest of Vespa owners and users; organize, protect, and supervise the activities of associated groups, with special interest in tourism; assist the various

groups in the technical and practical education of their membership, and lastly maintain ties with motoring and touring groups in Italy and elsewhere, establishing relationships of reciprocity...."

During the course of 1950 as well, the spread of Vespa Clubs continued at a dizzying pace. In the month of February, there were 45 associations. In the following two months, the number climbed to 55. And all of the clubs were always very active, especially in the north of Italy, where there were already forms of cooperation among the various cities, with exchanges, sister-city conventions, tours, and coordinated events. Among those, we should mention the great meet in Bologna, held on 20 and 21 May 1950, and the Women's Meet of San Remo, which took place the following July. No fewer than 250 female Vespa riders took part, to show the degree to which the Vespa was an instrument in the "emancipation" of women, who from the end of the war onward were demanding their rights of equality with men.

Beginning in 1951, the expansion of the Vespa Clubs phenomenon had an even sharper uptick, and soon was beyond restraint. Suffice it to note that there were no fewer than 20,000 Vespa riders who took part in the "Vespa Day" event, a super-meet involving twelve Italian cities.

Also in 1951, the spectacular "Bridge of Bassano Meet" (with the presence of all 106 Italian Vespa Clubs) took place. On that occasion, the event even took a political twist, with the presence of the clubs from Trieste and Trento, underscoring the desire of these two cities to remain united with Italy.

IF YOU LEAF THROUGH SPECIALTY MAGAZINES OF THE FIFTIES, THERE IS NOT AN ISSUE WITHOUT A REPORT ON AT LEAST ONE OF THE MANY MEETS ORGANIZED IN ITALY AND ABROAD. THE "SWARMS" WERE GIVEN SO MUCH SPACE THAT MANY COMPANIES BEGAN TO SPONSOR MEETS, JUST TO ASSOCIATE THEIR OWN NAME WITH THAT OF THE VESPA, THUS USING FOR THE FIRST TIME IN ITALY AN ADVERTISING CHANNEL THAT WAS STILL LARGELY UNEXPLORED.

The Vespa Clubs quickly became an international phenomenon. Associations similar to the one founded in Italy sprang up everywhere. On 7 February 1953, there was a conference in Milan attended by representatives of the Vespa Clubs of Belgium, France, Germany, Italy, Holland, and Switzerland, to found the Vespa Club of Europe; by general acclaim, Renzo Tassinari was named president. These, however, were not the only countries in which the passion for Vespa was on the rise. Surprising, the Vespa Club of England was quite active, and in 1956 it included no fewer than 3,000 members.

In terms of importance and originality, it is worth mentioning the major international Vespa event organized by the European Vespa Club. The event was held in Paris on 8 and 9 May 1951, and was particular noteworthy in that, in keeping with the dominant current affairs subject of the time, the Russian/American space race (just beginning), the procession featured a "Vespa Flying Saucer," with blinking lights, sirens, and training wheels, a monster that weighed many hundreds of pounds, thirteen feet across.

It is fair and safe to say: the Vespa, thanks to the various clubs, had finally attained stable orbit!

CLUBS

When we talk about the success of the Vespa, the phrase "in unity is our strength" is no mere commonplace. The Piaggio scooter owes a debt of gratitude to the various Vespa Clubs. Sales, in fact, began climbing immediately after the first meets. People seemed to want nothing more than to get together, travel, and have fun. From excursions to gymkhanas. Then came the first rallies, organized by no less than a founding organizer of the "Mille Miglia," Renzo Castagneto, who decided that Vespa enthusiasts could repeat the same course as the most famous Italian road race.

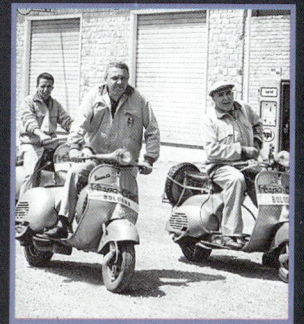

Renato Tassinari (photograph, top left) founded and promoted the Vespa Clubs, a "movement" in which many women also took part. Each meet or event drew at least a few hundred enthusiasts.

PART V

COMPETITION

RUN OR
YOU'RE
DONE FOR!

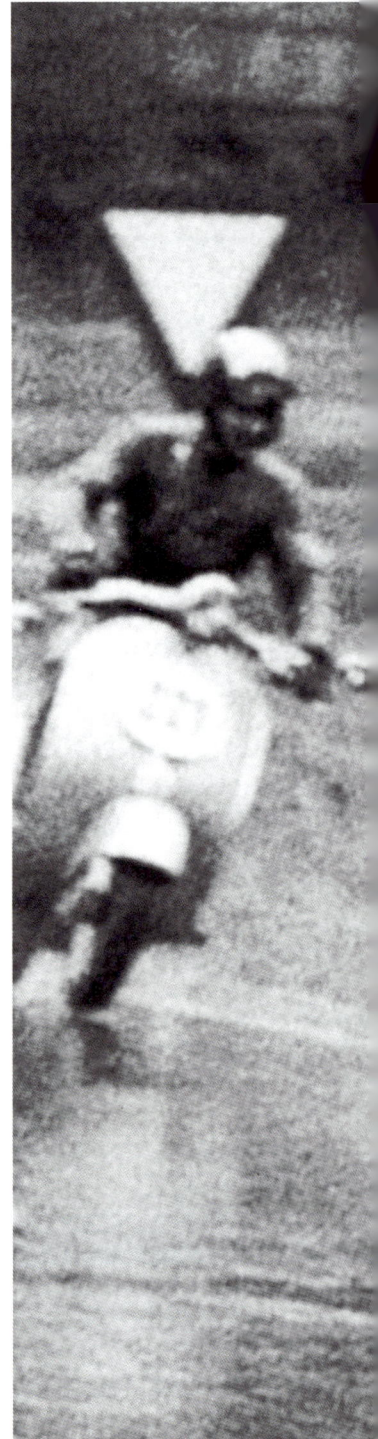

THE VESPA DID NOT ORIGINATE AS A RACING MACHINE BUT, IN SPITE OF PREDICTIONS TO THE CONTRARY, IT WOUND UP TRIUMPHING IN COMPETITION, ESPECIALLY IN RALLIES (LARGE PHOTO TO THE RIGHT). THE FIRST "VESPISTA" TO PARTICIPATE OFFICIALLY IN A "REAL" RACE WAS CARLO MACIOCCHI, IN APRIL 1947, IN THE "PRIMI PASSI" OF MILAN. HE CAME IN SECOND.

*T*he exciting story of the Vespa in competition began with an absolutely unconventional approach. The Piaggio company, in fact, never used special models to race, as was usually the case, but rather raced what were practically production models, all of which had therefore been extensively tested and proven directly by the mass market public. Considered by most as a runabout, the Vespa could not project much of a "racing" image, and seemed completely out of place in actual racing meets. The Vespa had little in common with true racing bikes, either in appearance or performance: its small wheels seemed unsuited to the challenges of the track, and the open-frame structure hardly seemed adequate to the thrust and stress involved in high-speed cornering and curves. The "vespisti," however, had no doubts at all. Right from the debut of the vehicle, in fact, there were those who were determined to turn their Vespas into little speedsters. Souped-up Vespas, then, generated a brand-new racing category, the "Sports Bar" entry, which produced all sorts of challenges, usually provoked by phrases such as: "My Vespa is faster than yours..." or else, even more often, "My Vespa can thrash your Lambretta..." The ritual was simple. Various minor modifications were made to the engines, and, when the home mechanic had run out of ideas, a red racing stripe was painted along the bodywork. The important thing was always to be tough!

After winning lots of informal races, Carlo Masciocchi decided, in April of 1947, to try to enter actual racing circuits by signing up his Vespa in the "Primi Passi" race of the Gentlemen Moto Club of Milan. The race inaugurated the season of endurance races with a grueling tour of the high valleys of the Bergamo area. Masciocchi came in second, delayed by a few spills and by the limited capacity of his little engine; still, it constituted a triumph for the Vespa because it proved that it could compete against even the toughest competitors. From that time on plenty of private racers began to compete in endurance races and gradually began to work their way up the finish rankings; in fact, at the end of its first season of competition the Vespa had a trophy cabinet featuring no fewer than 33 victories. The quality and quantity of racing successes achieved by private racers began to attract the notice of the Piaggio company;

encouraged by the enthusiasm of one of its two test drivers, Dino Mazzoncini, the company decided to form a small team of official racers. With this team, the Vespa competed in the following season in both endurance and sprint races. The first official victory came quickly, and it came in a speed race, on the Florence race track, in May of 1948. And it was not the last. That year was rich in racing successes. Among other distinctions, the team took first place (with all the competing Vespas crossing the finish line) in the "Trofeo dei Laghi," or 'Lakes Trophy,' a team competition covering a 600-kilometer course. In the "Sei Giorni Internazionale di Varese," or 'Varese International Six-Day race,' the most famous endurance race in Italy, the team came in second only because—according to the newspapers of the time—Mazzoncini was penalized for failing to stop at a checkpoint. New victories came with the first few months of 1949: in January the tireless Mazzoncini won a major victory on the Naples race track, while in the month of February the Piaggio scooter took another very unusual victory: the "motor-ski" race of Vicenza-Monte Gallio, for the "Alpengin" trophy, organized by the Moto Club di Berico. With the beginning of the endurance racing season, the Piaggio team began once again to reap victories: in April it won the "Primi Passi" or 'First Steps' trophy, with all three Vespa racers (Opessi, Spadini, and Castiglioni) reaching the finish line without penalties of any sort; next came the grueling series of races for the "Trofeo dell'Industria," or 'Industry Trophy,' occupying the team for the rest of the spring and summer season. The Italian Federation had broken down qualification for the trophy into three races: the "Scudo del Sud," or 'Shield of the South'; the "24 Ore," or '24 Hours'; and the "Mille Miglia," which ran over a total of 5,000 kilometers, with Vespa crisscross-

GYMKHANAS PROVED TO BE A POPULAR ALTERNATIVE TO RACING. THESE EVENTS SERVED TO HIGHLIGHT THE VESPA'S MANEUVRABILITY. HERE WE SEE A COMPETITOR FROM THE PIACENZA VESPA CLUB TACKLING A TIGHT CORNER UNDER THE VIGILANT EYE OF A CHILD-MARSHAL READY TO RAISE HIS RED FLAG TO SIGNAL ANY IRREGULARITY.

PURSUIT RACES WERE ANOTHER POPULAR "FORMULA": THESE COMPETITIONS, OFTEN AMATEUR EVENTS, WERE THE THEATER FOR LEGENDARY DUELS AMONG VESPAS AND LAMBRETTAS. IN THE PHOTO IN THE CENTER, TWO COMPETITORS ZIP THROUGH THE TWISTING STREETS OF CAGLIARI.

ing the entire Italian peninsula. Clearly this race made it possible to spread the Vespa gospel throughout the peninsula, even in southern Italy, where the Vespa was not as well known. The encouraging results of the Vespa's performance in the challenging trio of races can be understood in a few statistics: in the "Scudo del Sud," with six Vespas starting, five reached the finish line without penalties; Castiglioni was forced out of the race by mechanical problems. In the "24 Ore," six scooters started, and five reached the finish line without penalties; the unfortunate Castiglioni was once again forced to quit because of a spill. And in the "Milla Miglia," seven Vespas out of seven crossed the finish line without penalties; but Fassona and Castellini were disqualified because of a missing check-point stamp. On the whole, these results allowed Vespa to qualify in second place, five points behind the winner, in the "Trofeo dell'Industria." A considerable triumph, if we consider that the Vespa was racing

ENDURANCE RACES (IN WHICH "APE" PICKUP-SCOOTERS ALSO COMPETED) WERE THE MOST POPULAR EVENTS FOR SCOOTERISTS, EVEN IF THEY WERE MADE PARTICULARLY CHALLENGING BY THE ORGANIZERS. ABOVE, WE SEE THE TOUGH ADA PACE (WHO LATER BECAME A FAMOUS AUTOMOBILE RACER) RIDING HER VESPA AS SHE "FORDS" A MOUNTAIN STREAM ALONG THE COURSE OF THE FIRST VESPA PIEDMONTESE ENDURANCE CHAMPIONSHIP: THE DATE WAS 24 MAY 1953. ADA PACE PLACED EQUAL FIRST.

RIGHT: THE AUSTRIAN RACER TEILNEHMER DURING THE SHOFBERG-ROLLER RACE IN MAY 1958 (PHOTOGRAPH TAKEN FROM THE VERY HANDSOME BOOK, "VESPA MÌ AMORE," PUBLISHED IN GERMANY BY SCHRADER VERLAG).

against 250 cc. and 500 cc. motorcycles. The Vespa racing team continued its activities for a number of years and obtained numerous victories. To list them here would take too much space, and so we shall mention only the great triumph at the "Sei Giorni Internazionale di Varese," in 1951, crowning the Vespa once and for all as the best scooter in Italy. To gain some sense of the Vespa's edge over the competition, let us mention a few figures: out of the 218 vehicles that started, in fact, only 89 managed to complete the race without incurring penalties. Among the scooters, out of the 22 that started, 10 won the gold medal, and 9 of those were Vespas!

Over the course of the Fifties, however, the importance of official racing declined, since in 1952 the MV Agusta company entered the championship with a full-fledged Gran Prix bike with modified small wheels. The scooter manufacturers protested loudly for the loose interpretation of regulations, but as they were ignored by the racing authorities, they gradually began to stop entering the traditional competitions. Instead, Vespa created a series of single-marque competitions, beginning in 1951, and organized by the Vespa Club of Italy. Among these races, the first and unquestionably the most important was the "Mille Chilometri," or 'Thousand Kilometers' race organized by the Vespa Club of Brescia, under the guidance of Renzo Castagneto, who had first organized in 1927 the "Mille Miglia," race for cars. This

was definitely a grueling race, even though it was a single-marque event; it required the competitors to complete five legs of two hundred kilometers each, at an average speed of 50 kph. The final rank was determined by choosing two legs at random and taking into account the times and the overall penalties. Victory became all the more sought after because, aside from the honor and satisfaction of victory, there was a cash prize of 500,000 lire for the winner. From the first year on, entries arrived from all over Italy and from as far away as Belgium, France, and Germany, thus making it an international event. The race was held again on 5 July 1952, with the enthusiastic participation of 365 competitors from all over Europe. The audience was numerous, and excitedly watched the Vespas zipping along the route of the "Mille Miglia." At the starting line, the competitors were organized into 49 teams, each with 5 racers, representing the Vespa Clubs of as many cities, and 125 private racers. 354 riders crossed the finish line, with two tying for first place, Giovanni Furigo and Mario Pagain, while the Vicenza-based racer Zin inaugurated a tradition that would find many successors. He crossed the finish line with an average speed of 71.46 kph; he was disqualified but he still had the honor of being the fastest private "vespista." The daring Zin repeated his performance the following year. In fact, in the third edition of the "Mille Chilometri" (that year there were 372 competitors representing 76 Vespa Clubs), the six racers who were dis-

LEFT, ADA PACE AT THE STARTING LINE FOR THE "GIRO DEI TRE MARI" IN JULY 1956. IN THESE PAGES WE SEE A FEW SNAPSHOTS FROM HER RACING ALBUM. FAR LEFT, THIS PAGE, ADA PACE BEING CHEERED AT THE FINISH LINE OF THE "CRITERIUM VESPISTICO INTERNAZIONALE" (SHE FINISHED SECOND OVERALL IN 1955). ABOVE, AT THE MOTOVELODROMO TORINESE (MARCH 1953) IN A CHASE TRIAL CALLED THE "CACCIA ALLA VOLPE," LITERALLY 'FOX HUNT.' ON THE FACING PAGE, RIGHT, ADA PACE WITH HELMET IN HAND AND RADIO AROUND HER NECK, READY TO START IN THE "AUTO RADIO MOTO RADUNO," LITERALLY THE 'AUTO RADIO MOTORCYCLE MEET,' ON 27 APRIL 1952.

qualified included Zin and his imitators who raced "belly to the ground" and reached the finish line with average speeds of more than 72 kph. These "daredevils" were disqualified from the race by regulation but Castagneto and the Piaggio company, who were basically proud that anyone could drive a Vespa for a thousand kilometers at such high speeds, organized a special welcoming ceremony for them at five o'clock in the morning. The winner that year was Ezio Stenico of the Vespa Club of Trento, who took the prize of one million lire (the biggest prize in Italy for a motorcycle race of any kind), beating out Piero Bevilacqua of Imola. In 1953, another competition was established that was destined to add an epic dimension in the history of Vespa racing: the Vespa "Giro dei Tre Mari," literally 'Tour of the Three Seas.' This was a race run on an old bicycle racing course that had not been used since the end of the war, now revived for motorized vehicles. Piaggio chose to revive this race, which had always been particularly popular in the south of Italy, with a view to encouraging the popularity of the scooter in the southern regions, yet to be conquered by the new vehicle. The race was conceived as an endurance event, but the average required speed was set at

SPEED RECORDS WERE THE MOST EXCITING TEST BENCH FOR THE VESPA. THE VEHICLES USED WERE PREPARED SPECIALLY BY THE TESTING DIVISION OF THE PONTEDERA FIRM. ON THESE PAGES WE SEE THE ENDURANCE RECORD ATTEMPT MADE ON THE RACETRACK OF MONTHLÉRY IN THE MONTHS OF MARCH AND APRIL 1950. THE RIDERS MAZZONCINI, SPADONI (LATER REPLACED, AFTER AN ACCIDENT, BY ROMANO), MANAGED TO ROUND THE FRENCH RACETRACK AT VERY HIGH AVERAGES, WITH A PEAK SPEED OF 136.92 KPH, NEVER BEFORE ATTAINED.

50 kph, that is, the top speed allowed by international regulations; this meant that in many stretches of the race the competitors would have to zip along at 70 kph, not a very easy thing to do on roads that were often in extremely poor shape and in temperatures that were often African in nature (the race was run in July). The race, therefore, with its more-than 1,700 kilometers of length, then turned into a grueling competition, transforming a race for dilettantes accustomed to something on the order of fast touring, or "turismo veloce," into a real do-or-die battle. This, plus the constant presence of excited crowds along the course, turned the "Giro dei Tre Mari" into a popular success that is still remembered today. An illustrious unknown, representing a Vespa Club of any small town in Italy, could really kick out the jams, so to speak, facing the challenges of an extremely tough course and, if he managed to reach the finish line, he could zoom past cheering crowds lining the streets, urging him on as if he were one of the great champions of the "Mille Miglia." Both events continued their popularity over the years that followed, with an ever growing crowd of contestants, to the point that the various Vespa Clubs had to

begin selecting contestants at a local level, to limit the number of entries. Moreover, these races increasingly began to attract professional motorcycle racers such as Vighi, Opessi, and Spadoni, riders who had learned their skills on the roads of the "Mille Miglia" and the "Giro d'Italia."

During the early Fifties, Piaggio shifted its attention from official sprint and endurance races to the field of record-setting, where it meant to continue its tradition of questing to test the edge of the envelope that had distinguished its activity in the field of aeronautics. The first records that Vespa established in the registries maintained by the International Motorcycle Federation with headquarters in Pall Mall in London were set at Monthléry in 1950. A detailed account of this event exists, and was set down at the time by engineer Carlo Carbonero, who was in charge of the project, jointly with engineer Vittorio Casini. He noted that Piaggio wished to set records with its motorscooters that might serve to commemorate the technical progress that had been achieved, as well as helping to consolidate the scooter's remarkable popularity in world markets; and that this desire conflicted sharply with the difficulties of undertaking such an enterprise in the context of a compa-

ny that was straining every technical and manufacturing sinew to produce and constantly improve standard road vehicles. Despite this fact, record-setting Vespas could be and were readied and tested in the strictest secrecy, in the research and development sector. The research and testing done at Pontedera to obtain such high speeds from a 125 cc. engine were neither simple nor quick but, thanks to the experience accumulated during a number of years of endurance racing, the machine was ready to go by February 1950. The vehicle in question was a prototype that differed only slightly from the production model, even though the bodywork was entirely enclosed in a fairing and had a more streamlined silhouette. At this point, it became necessary to test it on the track where the records were to be set. With this end in mind, Mazzoncini and Spadoni set out for Monthléry with a "Vespa veloce." The tests were supposed to remain secret, but word got out, and many racing publications reported that the first, unsatisfactory tests were indications of a definitive failure. Despite these rumors, preparations for the attempt went on and, finally, on 23 March, a team of technicians headed by Carbonero and Casini with the test riders

AFTER THE RECORDS SET AT MONTHLÉRY (RIGHT AND FAR RIGHT, TWO MORE PICTURES FROM THAT TRACK) THE VESPA ALSO TOOK A WORLD SPEED RECORD FOR THE FLYING KILOMETER. THE SILURO (SHOWN IN THE PHOTO BELOW) RIDDEN BY DINO MAZZONCINI (RECOGNIZABLE IN THE PECULIAR AERODYNAMIC HELMET) RAN THE FLYING KILOMETER (IN THE STRETCH BETWEEN THE KM. 10 AND KM. 11 ON THE ROME-OSTIA HIGHWAY) AT A SPEED OF 171.102 KPH.

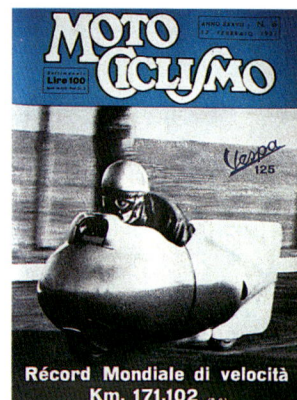

MOTO CICLISMO

Record Mondiale di velocità
Km. 171,102

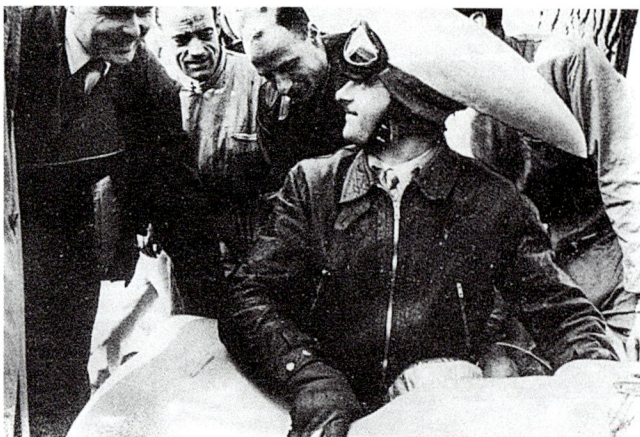

Mazzoncini, Castiglioni, and Spadoni set out for Monthléry with three specially calibrated Vespas, to make the final and official attempts. The beginning was not particularly promising: the morning of Wednesday 24 March dawned with barely acceptable atmospheric conditions. The wind was blowing hard when the Vespa began to turn laps around the track of Monthléry, the three test riders taking turns on the machines. A little after noon, Spadoni began to push his pace, maintaining a speed around the track averaging from 135 to 136 kph, but a bad spill destroyed his Vespa and forced him to withdraw. Spadoni was forced to return to Milan for an operation, and he was replaced by Bruno Romano. Despite the serious acci-

dent, the presence of a commissioner from the International Motorcycle Federation and a group of official timekeepers encouraged the Piaggio team to make an official record attempt; thus Mazzoncini and Castiglioni took turns riding for two hours, beating the existing records for the times involved. During the days that followed, the presence of strong winds prevented them from repeating the attempt, and it was not until 6 April that they were able to try again. Weather conditions were far from perfect but, as Carbonero himself confessed, the desire to return to Italy for Easter was so great that they decided to make another attempt, relying upon a drop in the wind in the late afternoon. At 3 pm they started the attempt, and the plan was to race for 10 hours. This meant riding late at night without any lighting except for oil lamps placed along the inner edge of the track. As Carbonero said later, "To recount ten hours of intense experience, spent minute by minute in hoping to succeed and the terror of seeing our plans collapse, is a difficult thing to do." In any case, the Vespa ran beautifully at an average speed of between 130 and 134 kph, with only one breakdown when the wire of a sparkplug pulled loose, requiring a four-minute pitstop and the loss of 7 km. from the average speed. Despite that, at 1:11 am on 7 April 1950, they clocked the results shown in the chart that follows.

Distance	kph	previous record
50 km	134,203	125,802
50 miles	134,573	126,059
100 km	134,733	126,701
1 hour	134,054	126,500
100 miles	127,777	121,350
2 hours	130,794	115,872
3 hours	125,713	107,314
4 hours	123,376	108,304
500 km	123,463	108,504
5 hours	124,065	107,856
6 hours	124,636	107,975
500 miles	123,919	107,182
7 hours	124,056	107,182
8 hours	124,274	107,386
1000 km	124,306	103,507
9 hours	123,434	107,556
10 hours	123,537	104,912

Fastest lap at an average speed of 136.92 kph

In 1951 Piaggio decided to attempt to set the most sought-after and demanding speed record: the flying kilometer. If the Vespa had proved its capacity for endurance at Monthléry, now it would have to prove that

ONE OF THE NUMEROUS VESPAS PREPARED BY THE PIAGGIO RACING DIVISION TO TAKE PART IN CIRCUIT SPEED RACES (LEFT). NOTE THE ENLARGED FUEL TANK, WHICH ALSO GAVE THE RACER THE SUPPORT HE NEEDED TO ASSUME THE MOST AERODYNAMIC POSITION. THE FRONT SHIELD WAS GIVEN A BRAND-NEW FAIRING CONFIGURATION.

it was unbeatable in pure speed, becoming the fastest motorscooter on earth. The flying kilometer was, infact, considered the most important record in terms of publicity and advertising, because it meant the most in technical terms. In a meeting that Enrico Piaggio held with his team of technicians, engineers, and managers, it was decided—on the basis of previous experience—to develop a vehicle that would synthesize all of the technical and racing achievements of the Vespa. The engineers assigned to the project were Corradino D'Ascanio and Vittorio Casini. This time the result was a rolling torpedo that was at best a distant cousin of the production Vespa. The frame consisted of a single metal beam that joined the wheels and allowed the rider to assume a particularly aerodynamic position, competely enclosed by the streamlined fairing. The engine was still a two-stroke and, according to the claims of Piaggio at the time, it had water-cooled split-cylinders, with dual carburetors, and fueled by an alcohol-and-oil 12 percent mixture. Actually, it was an engine with opposed cylinders, covered by the most rigorous veil of secrecy: it was considered more impressive to obtain such performance with a split-cylinders engine.

As the years passed, however, it became less and less necessary to defend this "fib." In any case, whether it was with split-cylinders or opposed cylinders, on the morning of 9 February 1951, the Vespa Siluro (literally, 'torpedo'), ridden by Dino Mazzoncini, set the world speed record for the flying kilometer between kilometer 10 and kilometer 11 of the Rome-Ostia highway. The

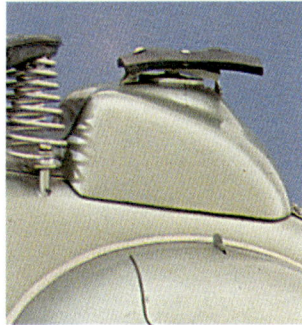

record was set with a single attempt (out and back) that proved immediately successful. The average speed of 171 kph in fact easily outpaced the existing record, set during the Mondial with a motorscooter named Mondial and ridden by Gino Cavanna. In the first pass, from Rome toward Ostia, the Piaggio scooter established a time of 20.64 seconds, for an average speed of 174.418 kph; in the second pass, on the way back, the Vespa traveled at an average speed of 169.91 kph, with a time of 21.44 seconds.

The average speed then was exactly 171.102 kph (equivalent to 106 mph) and the average time was 21.4 seconds. Clearly, this was an important record, and in fact other major scooter makers immediately set about trying to beat it; in the end the Innocenti company managed to do so with a Lambretta that was pushed to a speed of 202 kph. Later, however, an accident that took the life of the test rider Renato Magi when he was trying to beat that record on an MV scooter discouraged practically everyone from making any more attempts.

THE VESPA THAT WON NINE GOLD MEDALS IN THE "SEI GIORNI INTERNAZIONALE" IN 1951. YOU CAN SEE THE MODIFICATIONS MADE TO THE SUSPENSION, THE MUDGUARD, AND THE HEADLIGHT. A SPARE TIRE AND EXTRA FUEL TANK WERE ALSO ADDED

125 SPORT PROTOTIPO

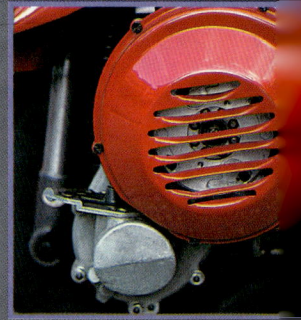

A Vespa racing speedster? Why not? In 1948, the two Politano brothers, who owned a Vespa dealership in Cosenza, equipped the Piaggio scooter with an ultralight and "aerodynamic" body, with a view to winning races in the national championship, and they actually did score several victories. The "visible" engine with a larger carburetor and straight through exhaust was modified directly by Piaggio itself. The 125 Sport Prototipo, or 'prototype,' had a special fuel tank for rapid filling, integrated with the anatomically shaped seat.

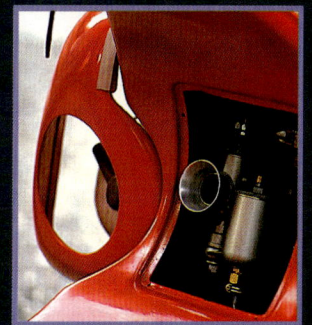

Engine: horizontal two-stroke single-cylinder, 124.85 cc. displacement, 6 hp at 6,000 rpm, Dell'Orto 22 carburetor, three-speed gearbox, lubrication with 10 percent mixture, top speed 95 kph.

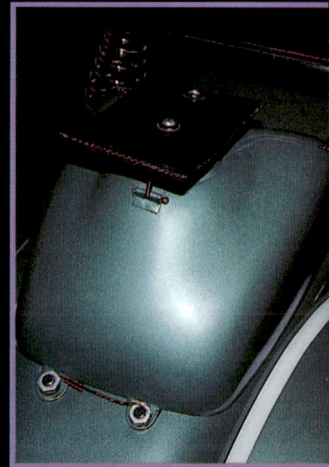

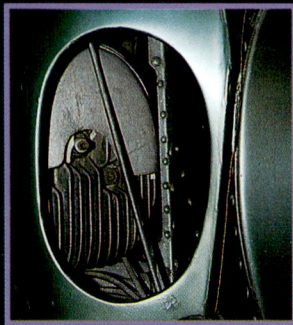

Engine: horizontal two-stroke single-cylinder, 124.85 cc. displacement, 7 hp at 6,750 rpm, Dell'Orto 23 mm. carburetor, three-speed gearbox, lubrication with 10 percent mixture, top speed 95 kph.

125 SEI GIORNI

THIS IS THE VESPA MOST SOUGHT-AFTER BY COLLECTORS: THE LEGENDARY "SEI GIORNI," OR 'SIX DAYS,' NAMED AFTER THE GRUELING ENDURANCE RACE IN WHICH IT COMPETED SUCCESSFULLY IN 1951, WINNING NUMEROUS GOLD MEDALS. ONLY A FEW HUNDRED EXAMPLES WERE BUILT, AND IT STANDS OUT FOR ITS ESPECIALLY STURDY FRAME, DESIGNED FOR ENDURANCE RACING AND OFF-ROAD USE. THE MOST NOTABLE FEATURE IS THE EXTRA-LARGE FUEL TANK, SET BEHIND THE SEAT, WITH A SPECIAL SUPPORT TO ALLOW THE RIDER TO STRETCH OUT FULL-LENGTH AT SPEED.

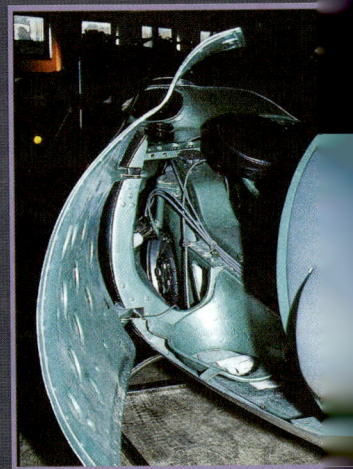

Engine: two-stroke opposed twin cylinders, water-cooled, dual-carburetor, alcohol and oil 12 percent mixture.

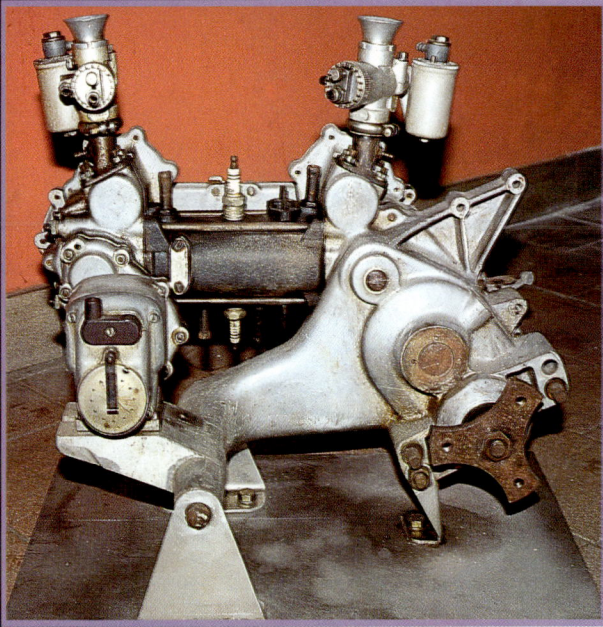

Vespa
SILURO

1951, ROME-OSTIA HIGHWAY. IN THIS REMARKABLE SILVERY TORPEDO, ON THE MORNING OF 9 FEBRUARY, THE RACER DINO MAZZONCINI SET A NEW WORLD SPEED RECORD FOR THE FLYING KILOMETER: 171 KPH.

90 SUPER SPRINT

TAKING THE NEWBORN "CINQUANTI NO," OR 'LITTLE FIFTY,' AS A STARTING POINT THE PONTEDERA FIRM, DESIGNED A "SPORTIER" NEW MODEL: THUS, IN 1966, THE VESPA 90 SUPER SPRINT APPEARED. THIS WAS VERY RARE AND DISTINCTIVE MODEL, DISTINGUISHED IN PARTICULAR BY THE UNUSUAL GLOVEBOX SET BETWEEN THE SEAT AND THE HANDLEBARS, CLOSING THE CENTRAL SPACE OF THE BODYWORK. THE **90 SS** HAD A PARTICULARLY NARROW HANDLEBAR, A POINTED MUDGUARD, AND A SPARE WHEEL (SET BETWEEN THE RIDER'S LEGS) WITH HUBCAPS THE SAME COLOR AS THE BODYWORK. A SPORTY BUT ELEGANT VEHICLE!

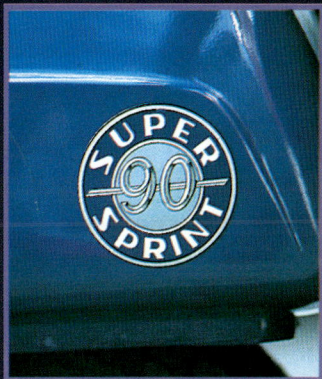

Engine: horizontal two-stroke single-cylinder, 88.5 cc. displacement, 6 hp at 6,000 rpm, Dell'Orto SHB 16 carburetor, four-speed gearbox, lubrication with 2 percent mixture, top speed 93 kph.

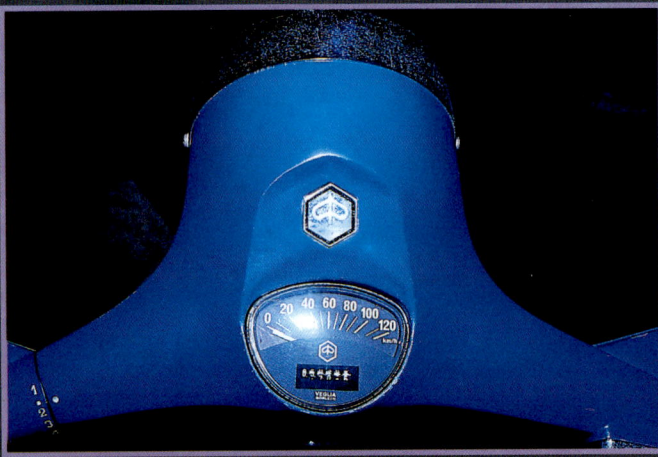

Engine: horizontal two-stroke single-cylinder, 180.7 cc. displacement, 10.4 hp at 5,700 rpm, Dell'Orto 20 mm. carburetor, four-speed gearbox, lubrication with 2 percent mixture, top speed 106 kph.

180 RALLY

CREATED IN 1968, FOR MANY YEARS THIS WAS THE MOST POWERFUL AND FASTEST SCOOTER AROUND. NEVER BEFORE HAD PIAGGIO BUILT SUCH A HIGH-PERFORMANCE VESPA. FORERUNNER OF THE EVEN MORE POWERFUL 200 RALLY, IT BOASTS MORE THAN 10 HORSEPOWER, LETTING IT ZIP ALONG EASILY AT MORE THAN 100 KILOMETERS PER HOUR. COMPARED WITH THE PREVIOUS 180 SS, IT HAD A MORE MODERN BODYWORK (NO MOULDINGS) AND A MORE POWERFUL ENGINE (WITH ROTARY INTAKE VALVE).

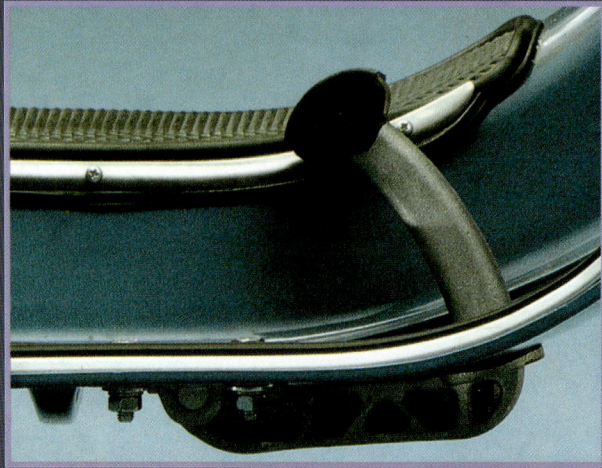

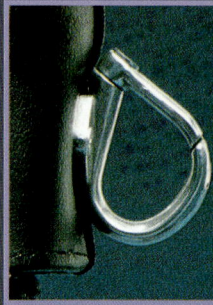

Engine: horizontal two-stroke single-cylinder, 121.2 cc. displacement, 5.6 hp at 5,500 rpm, Dell'Orto 19 mm. carburetor, four-speed gearbox, lubrication with 2 percent mixture, top speed 85 kph.

125 PRIMAVERA

IN ABSOLUTE TERMS, THIS IS ONE OF THE MOST SUCCESSFUL AND POPULAR MODELS OF VESPA. IT APPEARED IN 1967 BUT IT ENJOYED ITS BOOM IN THE EARLY SEVENTIES WHEN IT BECAME TRENDY AMONG THE SIXTEEN-YEAR-OLDS OF THE TIME. MORE THAN 220,000 OF THESE VESPAS WERE SOLD, GIVING SOME IDEA OF ITS POPULARITY. EXCELLENT PERFORMANCE AND BRILLIANT STYLING (ESPECIALLY IN WHITE) ALLOWED IT TO SELL STEADILY WITH VIRTUALLY NO CHANGES FOR MANY YEARS. IT WAS FLANKED BY THE MORE POWERFUL ET3 SERIES (ELECTRONIC, 3 INTAKE PORTS).

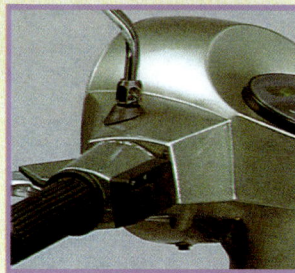

Engine: horizontal two-stroke single-cylinder, 123.4 cc. displacement, 8.5 hp at 6,700 rpm, Dell'Orto 16 mm. carburetor, four-speed gearbox, lubrication with 2 percent mixture, top speed 95 kph

WHEN THE "NEW LINE" WAS INTRODUCED IN 1978, THIS IS THE FORM IT TOOK. EVERYONE WAS WAITING TO SEE WHAT PIAGGIO WOULD PRODUCE IN THIS MAJOR CHANGE. THE RESULT? PERFECT: A VESPA WITH LINES SO HANDSOME THAT IT IS STILL BEING SOLD, VIRTUALLY UNCHANGED, TWENTY YEARS LATER. COMPARED WITH THE SEVENTIES MODELS, THE MAIN IMPROVEMENTS CONCERN THE SUSPENSION, WHILE AT THE END OF THE NINETIES IT WAS EQUIPPED WITH A FRONT DISK BRAKE. THIS IS STILL AN OFFICIAL PIAGGIO PRODUCT EVEN IN THE THIRD MILLENNIUM, SHOWING THAT IT IS POSSIBLE TO OWN A CLASSIC VESPA BY BUYING IT NEW FROM A DEALERSHIP.

125 PX

THE NUMBERS

THE FIRST TEN YEARS OF THE VESPA

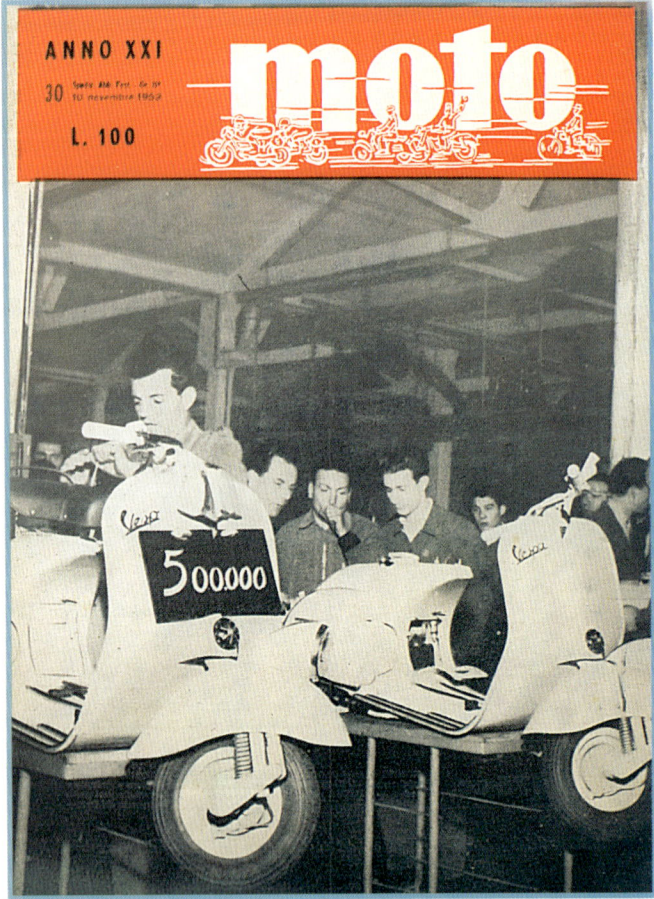

N umbers can help us to understand how a legend is born and grows. The numbers of the Vespa tell us that success, in the first ten years of life, came progressively, constantly. There were no earthquakes, no surges, but there were also no plunges. The Vespa then sank roots into the market like a slow-growing oak tree, deep and solid. No other scooter manufacturer was able to do the same. Not even Innocenti, which was certainly offering serious competition to Piaggio. When competition from the auto industry strengthened to a gale that swept away everything else, the other marques began to dim and, sadly, die out. The Vespa, on the other hand, made use of the same winds to kindle fires in other parts of the world.

After 1971, the Piaggio scooter was in fact the only sur-

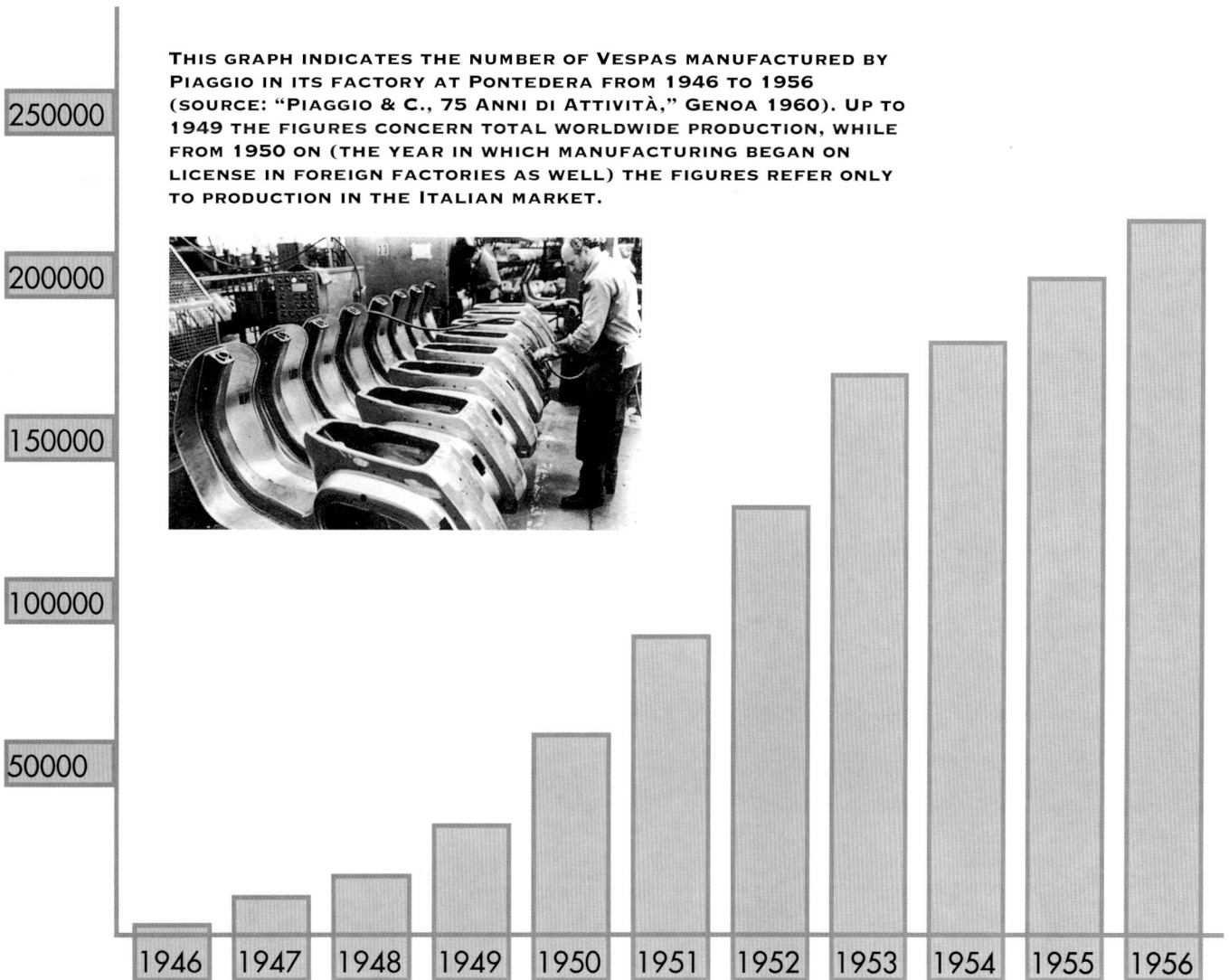

THIS GRAPH INDICATES THE NUMBER OF VESPAS MANUFACTURED BY PIAGGIO IN ITS FACTORY AT PONTEDERA FROM 1946 TO 1956 (SOURCE: "PIAGGIO & C., 75 ANNI DI ATTIVITÀ," GENOA 1960). UP TO 1949 THE FIGURES CONCERN TOTAL WORLDWIDE PRODUCTION, WHILE FROM 1950 ON (THE YEAR IN WHICH MANUFACTURING BEGAN ON LICENSE IN FOREIGN FACTORIES AS WELL) THE FIGURES REFER ONLY TO PRODUCTION IN THE ITALIAN MARKET.

vivor on the marketplace. But it was not mere good luck that ensured its survival. Nor was it the scooter's unquestioned technical qualities or stupendous design (the Vespa, like Pininfarina's Cisitalia, is part of the permanent collection of the Museum of Modern Art in New York). What counted more, perhaps, as we have seen, was the positive and captivating image that Piaggio managed to construct over the years around this product. The Vespa Clubs were important. Advertising was important. But the real winning card was Piaggio's capacity to interpret the times and to reinvent the Vespa over and over again in accordance with people's expectations. An operation that continues successfully to the present day.

The statistics that follow concern production of the Vespa from 1949 to 1959, documenting the trend of that success. The numbers shown below refer to production from the Pontedera plant only, and do not include production by foreign licensees (which began in 1950).

1946

PRODUCTION OF THE VESPA 98 BEGAN IN MARCH 1946, EVEN BEFORE A PATENT WAS ISSUED FOR THE SCOOTER. FROM THE MONTH OF MAY, INSTEAD, PRODUCTION BEGAN ON THE FIRST RIGID-TYPE 125 MODEL, DESIGNED FOR EXPORT.

98

MONTH	ASSEMBLED	TESTED	FINISHED	IN STOCK	SHIPPED		
					domestic	international	Total
March	10	9	9	-	9	-	9
April	20	15	15	-	15	-	15
May	45	42	42	-	42	-	42
June	140	130	130	-	130	-	130
July	150	145	143	4	141	-	141
August	280	272	272	-	276	-	276
September	415	408	408	29	379	-	379
October	435	404	404	56	377	-	377
November	476	436	436	142	350	-	350
December	539	605	605	119	628	-	628

125 *rigid-type*

MONTH	ASSEMBLED	TESTED	FINISHED	IN STOCK	SHIPPED		
					domestic	international	Total
May	3	3	3	-	-	3	3
June	-	-	-	-	-	-	-
July	7	7	7	2	-	5	5
August	15	15	15	1	-	16	16
September	3	3	3	-	-	4	4
October	2	2	2	-	-	2	2
November	74	64	64	53	-	11	11
December	61	71	71	28	-	96	96

THE YEAR 1947 BROUGHT THE FIRST POSITIVE RESULTS. FOR THE VESPA 98 GROWTH WAS ALMOST ALWAYS CONSTANT, FOR THE RIGID-TYPE 125 PROGRESS WAS HALTING, AND IN THE MONTH OF APRIL NOT A SINGLE 125 WAS BUILT.

1947

98

MONTH	ASSEMBLED	TESTED	FINISHED	IN STOCK	SHIPPED		
					domestic	international	Total
January	510	385	385	137	367	-	367
February	428	371	470	181	426	-	426
March	696	414	515	52	644	-	644
April	430	604	604	46	610	-	610
May	500	536	480	149	377	-	377
June	539	592	592	78	663	-	663
July	737	771	788	39	827	-	827
August	847	793	773	44	767	-	767
September	993	992	992	41	995	-	995
October	1318	1226	1285	5	1321	-	1321
November	1223	1315	1315	-	1320	-	1320
December	1352	1351	1250	101	1149	-	1149

THE 1947 VESPA 98, WITH METAL LUGGAGE RACK; AN ACCESSORY OF THE TIME.

125 *rigid-type*

MONTH	ASSEMBLED	TESTED	FINISHED	IN STOCK	SHIPPED domestic	international	Total
January	102	69	69	24	-	73	73
February	60	79	79	103	-	-	-
March	79	40	40	19	-	124	124
April	-	1	1	10	-	10	10
May	270	260	260	118	-	152	152
June	42	63	63	151	-	30	30
July	177	182	182	8	-	325	325
August	108	76	107	-	-	115	115
September	207	208	204	-	-	204	204
October	2	33	30	25	-	5	5
November	20	20	12	31	-	6	6
December	50	50	40	69	-	2	2

1948

THE YEAR 1948 WAS AN IMPORTANT ONE FOR VESPA WHICH WAS NOW EQUIPPED WITH FRONT SUSPENSION, AND WAS POWERED BY A **125 CC.** ENGINE THROUGHOUT THE RANGE. THE OLD MODELS DID REMAIN IN PRODUCTION UNTIL THE MONTH OF MARCH TO FULFILL OUTSTANDING ORDERS.

98

MONTH	ASSEMBLED	TESTED	FINISHED	IN STOCK	SHIPPED domestic	international	Total
January	1345	1390	1410	23	1488	-	1488
February	1434	1361	1366	-	1389	-	1389
March	169	354	430	89	341	-	341

125 *rigid-type*

MONTH	ASSEMBLED	TESTED	FINISHED	IN STOCK	SHIPPED domestic	international	Total
January	-	-	30	34	-	65	65
February	-	-	-	28	-	6	6
March	575	575	575	-	119	484	603

MONTH	ASSEMBLED	TESTED	FINISHED	IN STOCK	SHIPPED		
					domestic	international	Total
January	207	215	194	10	194	4	198
February	2	2	2	-	2	-	2
March	180	157	144	-	111	33	144
April	1520	1493	1457	-	1441	16	1457
May	1652	1601	1607	7	1399	1	1400
June	1518	1430	1430	4	1433	-	1433
July	2017	2034	2027	2	2028	1	2029
August	1396	1626	1604	27	1543	36	1579
September	1992	2004	2011	36	1871	131	2002
October	1933	1955	1951	8	1861	118	1979
November	1773	1801	1800	49	1516	243	1759
December	1790	1805	1784	22	1642	185	1827

THE "APE" (LITERALLY 'BEE') MINI-TRUCK WAS A MEMBER OF THE EXTENDED VESPA FAMILY. IT WAS CREATED BY PIAGGIO IN 1947 TO MEET THE DEMAND FOR LIGHT COMMERCIAL TRANSPORT. THE "APE" SHOWN HERE IS A VARIATION ON THE THEME: THE "CALESSINO," OR CALASH BUGGY. THIS PARTICULAR VEHICLE WAS USED ESPECIALLY AS A TAXI IN SEASIDE RESORTS SUCH AS CAPRI OR RICCIONE. THE REAR SEAT COULD EASILY ACCOMMODATE TWO PEOPLE OR, WITH A BIT OF A SQUEEZE, THREE.

1949

FROM THE APRIL OF 1949, ONLY THE VESPA 125 WITH SUSPENSION REMAINED IN PRODUCTION. ONLY 575 SCOOTERS WERE PRODUCED WITH THE RIGID-TYPE FRAME, AND 119 OF THOSE WERE TRANSFORMED INTO 98 CC. MODELS FOR THE ITALIAN MARKET

125

MONTH	ASSEMBLED	TESTED	FINISHED	IN STOCK	SHIPPED		
					domestic	international	Total
January	1940	1851	1850	64	1802	6	1808
February	1820	1911	1913	140	1823	14	1837
March	2330	2257	2307	32	2413	2	2415
April	2334	2272	2302	16	2142	176	2318
May	2854	2883	2813	20	2719	90	2809
June	3178	3191	3227	110	3040	97	3137
July	3682	3641	3550	-	3443	217	3660
August	2924	3080	3200	34	3906	160	3166
September	3950	3877	3900	153	3590	191	3781
October	2779	2745	2707	93	2696	71	2767
November	3953	3902	3909	148	3814	40	3854
December	3999	4049	4000	615	3530	3	3533

THE 1949 VESPA 125; NOTE THE TINY BUMPER ON THE FRONT MUDGUARD.

IN 1950 PRODUCTION CONTINUED TO GROW.
FRENCH AND BRITISH LICENSEES BEGAN TO
MANUFACTURE VESPAS ABROAD; IN THE MONTHS
OF NOVEMBER AND DECEMBER, RESPECTIVELY,
1,600 AND 2,200 MODELS WERE BUILT IN
UNASSEMBLED PARTS, FOR ASSEMBLY IN FRANCE.

1950

125

MONTH	ASSEMBLED	TESTED	FINISHED	IN STOCK	SHIPPED		
					domestic	international	Total
January	4019	3946	4000	748	3822	45	3867
February	4011	4004	4000	332	3873	543	4416
March	4744	4829	4800	2	4519	611	5130
April	5099	5079	5102	50	4691	393	5054
May	5425	5461	5400	1	4952	496	5449
June	5199	5236	5292	30	4833	832	5263
July	5757	5766	5700	38	3944	859	5692
August	4333	4287	4305	69	4850	330	4274
September	5846	5887	5900	198	4090	621	5471
October	4543	4627	4600	331	1301	677	4767
November	4943	4985	5047	3424	3810	653	1954
December	2628	2588	2572	3629	2200	157	2057

1951

THE FIRST TWO MONTHS OF 1951 WERE MARKED BY A LONG SERIES OF STRIKES WHICH SLOWED PRODUCTION AT PIAGGIO. BEGINNING IN MARCH, HOWEVER, THERE WAS IMMEDIATELY A SHARP UPTURN, MATERIALIZING INTO A PEAK PRODUCTION OF 7,843 VESPAS MANUFACTURED IN JULY

125

MONTH	ASSEMBLED	TESTED	FINISHED	IN STOCK	SHIPPED		
					domestic	international	Total
January	3054	3039	3000	3303	2984	352	3336
February	4804	4706	4650	2232	4861	860	5721
March	6436	6399	6400	288	6556	1788	8344
April	6338	6321	6300	191	4954	1459	6413
May	7009	6986	7000	244	5835	1112	6947
June	7254	7258	7250	199	5612	1683	7295
July	7843	7986	7846	7	6673	1365	8038
August	5640	5711	5786	145	4978	670	5648
September	7586	7557	7500	203	5813	1629	7442
October	6347	6346	6380	885	5023	674	5697
November	7525	7474	7500	2961	3852	1572	5424
December	6915	6901	6856	4981	2857	1979	4836

THE 1951 MODEL OF THE VESPA 125 NO LONGER HAD "ROD" STYLE GEAR SHIFTS

In 1952 as well substantial increases in Vespa production occurred. Also worth noting is that the 53 model was presented in November, while beginning in December the "Utilitaria" (or 'runabout') version began production (53 U).

1952

125

MONTH	ASSEMBLED	TESTED	FINISHED	IN STOCK	SHIPPED		
					domestic	international	Total
January	7900	7900	7900	8533	3424	924	4348
February	8000	8000	8000	10624	4449	1460	5909
March	7977	8000	8000	9787	6542	2287	8829
April	7600	7600	7680	8919	7201	1352	8553
May	7968	8000	8000	10096	4660	2167	6827
June	7392	7373	7360	9686	5759	2011	7770
July	7842	7855	7853	1343	11039	5157	16196
August	4143	4262	4208	636	3205	1710	4915
September	7596	7449	7500	163	5706	2294	8000
October	7524	7472	7480	851	6493	272	6765
November	5832	6001	5958	2250	1247	3308	4555
December	7230	7136	7222	2246	2246	2140	7226

1953

IN JANUARY OF 1953 THE
CLASSIFICATION CRITERIA FOR THE
DATA SHOWN HERE CHANGED.
BEGINNING IN FEBRUARY OF 1953,
PRODUCTION NUMBERS WERE SIMPLY
LUMPED INTO A SINGLE CATEGORY
FOR "VESPAS PRODUCED."
ALONGSIDE, THE VESPA 125 U OF
1953.

MONTH	VESPA
January	8224
February	7222
March	7340
April	8549
May	9272
June	9220
July	10283
August	6573
September	9280
October	7864
November	8126
December	8755
TOTAL	100708

1954

THE YEAR 1954 MARKED THE
ENTRY OF TWO NEW MODELS
DESTINED FOR GREAT SUCCESS: THE
VESPA WITH THE NEW 150 CC.
MOTOR AND, IN THE MONTH OF
OCTOBER, THE FIRST TEN UNITS OF
THE SPORTIER 150 GRAN SPORT
WERE MANUFACTURED.

MONTH	VESPA 125	VESPA 150	VESPA GS	ALL VESPAS
January	9164	-	-	9164
February	9501	-	-	9501
March	10310	-	-	10310
April	9990	-	-	9990
May	9642	-	-	9642
June	9089	-	-	9089
July	9469	-	-	9469
August	5192	-	-	5192
September	9491	-	-	9491
October	7861	608	-	8439
November	4854	3520	-	8374
December	5748	3045	10	8803
TOTAL	100287	7173	10	107470

MONTH	VESPA 125	VESPA 150	VESPA GS	ALL VESPAS
January	132	8268	50	8450
February	-	8326	90	8416
March	-	9331	413	9744
April	976	6454	740	8170
May	4090	3655	1160	8905
June	4534	2296	1500	8330
July	5862	1858	1358	9078
August	2969	1808	813	5590
September	4973	3560	1400	9933
October	3843	4016	1441	9300
November	2821	4458	1496	8775
December	5190	2767	1186	9143
TOTAL	35390	56797	11647	103834

1955

THE YEAR 1955 WITNESSED A SUBSTANTIAL CONSOLIDATION OF THE NEW MODELS AND A DECLINE IN THE OLD VERSIONS OF THE 125; IN THE MONTH OF JANUARY ONLY 132 UNITS OF THE OLD 125 WERE BUILT.

MONTH	VESPA 125	VESPA 150	VESPA GS	ALL VESPAS
January	5318	4226	479	10020
February	4579	5061	144	9784
March	4788	5493	20	10301
April	4192	5219	322	9733
May	3208	5998	1251	10457
June	2545	6747	1400	10692
July	3567	6708	1575	11850
August	1693	4262	821	6776
September	3356	5972	1437	10765
October	4484	5871	1407	11762
November	4060	5478	1312	10850
December	3520	4552	1428	9500
TOTAL	45310	65587	11596	122493

1956

THE YEAR 1956 SAW THE DEBUT OF THE VESPA GS: SALES, AFTER THE INEVITABLE BREAKING-IN PERIOD, SETTLED AT IMPRESSIVE LEVELS. THE BULK OF THE PRODUCTION OF COURSE REMAINED WITH THE "TWO-WHEEL RUNABOUTS."

THE FUTURE

VESPA AND PIAGGIO FLYING BEYOND YEAR 2000

So we are in the 21st century! We have talked about this so many times that we can hardly believe we are finally here. To say 2000 has always meant something far, far away, still to be invented, still to be discovered. But now that we are here, with a certain element of surprise we realize that many of those things that we have imagined and expected have completely failed to materialize.

Where are the cars with fins and plexiglas bubbles, zipping around like little flying saucers? And there are no roads hovering in midair, connecting one skyscraper and the next. Men and women are not wearing sheaths, or metallic overalls. And most important, nobody would dream of popping a pill intead of sitting down to a plate of spaghetti. Those futurologists who described the earth as if it were Mars, then, really got it all wrong. The world has moved in a completely different direction, changing to be sure, but not in the direction we expected. Unbridled imagination was replaced by concreteness and prac-

THE PIAGGIO COMPANY HAS LONG BEEN ON A CONTINUAL QUEST FOR NEW IDEAS. AMONG THE LATEST GENERATION OF PRODUCTS IS THE HEXAGON, A DISTILLATE OF COMFORT, LUXURY, TRANSPORT CAPACITY, AND ERGONOMICS (ABOVE, AN EARLY SKETCH). ON THE RIGHT, A TRIBUTE TO A PAST OF WHICH PIAGGIO IS STILL PROUD: THE VESPA 50, OF WHICH 3,000 NUMBERED UNITS WERE SPECIALLY MANUFACTURED IN 1991 TO COMMEMORATE THE REVOLUTIONARY "CINQUANTINO" OF THE SIXTIES.

WOMEN HAVE ALWAYS BEEN PART OF THE VESPA IMAGE, AND THE VESPA HAS REPAID THE FAVOR, STRIDING ALONGSIDE WOMEN IN THEIR BATTLE FOR EMANCIPATION. NOW THAT THE GOAL HAS BEEN REACHED, GIRLS WAVE THE VESPA AS A BANNER. "CIAO, ROBERTO, I AM COMING TO PICK YOU UP ON MY VESPA..." THE GIRL SEEMS TO BE SAYING ON THE PAY PHONE. TIMES CHANGE, BUT NOT THE VESPA...

ticality. And many things, the best ones of course, have persisted and survived. Some things have even remained exactly as they were. Among them, the Vespa, a legend that has managed to survive long beyond others that seemed equally indestructible, like those of the Volkswagen Beetle and the Citröen 2CV. All that has changed is the approach. The candor and the simplicity with which the Vespa presented itself to the Italians more than fifty years ago, would not find the same welcome today. The product, as the jargon would call it, has become mature and the vision that the new generations have of it is completely different. The Vespa now constitutes a technically sophisticated, specialized vehicle, complementary to the car, no longer an alternative to it. Its most appealing quality is that it is ideal for city traffic. Its image is incredibly young and fresh. But above all it is no longer a local phenomenon, an element that—as we said at the beginning—is indistinguishable from the Italian landscape. It is now international in its placement. The Vespa is everywhere.

What was the secret that allowed such a decisive metamorphosis? Certainly, the capacity to be reborn on a constant basis, while always remaining identical and unchanged. Piaggio, starting out with one miracle, has

THE VESPA IS SYNONYMOUS WITH "FRESHNESS," THANKS TO ITS POPULARITY AMONG YOUNG PEOPLE WHO CONSIDER IT THEIR FAVORITE VEHICLE. IN THE PAST, WE SAID, THE VESPA WAS PART OF THE RURAL LANDSCAPE OF ITALY; NOW IT IS AN INEVITABLE PRESENCE IN THE ITALIAN URBAN LANDSCAPE. AND IF THERE WAS A TIME WHEN PEOPLE TRANSPORTED ENTIRE FAMILIES ON THE OLD VESPA, NOWADAYS IT IS PRIMARILY YOUNG PEOPLE WHO CHOOSE IT AS THEIR STALWART COMPANION, WHEN IT IS NOT ACTUALLY "DOUBLE-DATING" IN LINE WITH A TRADITIONAL PIAGGIO PHILOSOPHY, SO MUCH SO THAT IT BECAME A SUCCESSFUL ADVERTISING SLOGAN: "CHI VESPA MANGIA LE MELE..." LITERALLY 'IF YOU VESPA, YOU WILL HAVE A BITE OF THE APPLE..."

worked a second miracle. What it has done is to give more and more body to the spirit that triggered the birth of the Vespa: offering the public practical vehicles, reliable and technologically advanced, which would fit with the real needs of people. And properly interpreting various historic moments, it added new ideas to existing ideas. The Vespa family has thus grown.

The range of vehicles (further enriched by the acquisition of new and prestigious labels such as Gilera) now includes more than 50 models, including mopeds, scooters, and vehicles with three or four wheels, with a wide range of engines. And since ecology is a current topic, there is now a Vespa driven by an electric motor!

And with the brand-new ET 4 with a four-cycle engine, Vespa is ready to satisfy the most stringent anti-pollution regulations. But Piaggio too has "expanded." The main manufacturing plant of course is still the one at Pontedera,

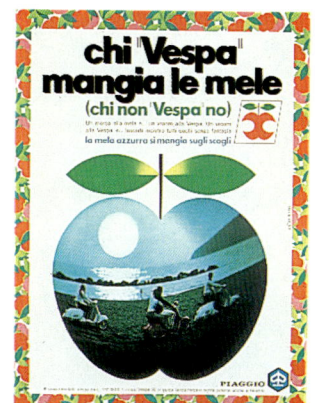

PIAGGIO IS PREPARING TO ENTER THE LARGEST MARKET IN THE WORLD: CHINA, WHERE A SUPER-MODERN FACTORY IS ALREADY IN OPERATION. THE PIAGGIO LYMAN FOSHAN MOTORCYCLE PLANT IS SHOWN HERE. IN THE MEANWHILE, PREPARATIONS ARE UNDERWAY TO LAUNCH A NEW PRODUCT: THE SFERA WITH A FOUR-STROKE ENGINE.

with the largest and most modern factory in Europe for the production of two-wheeled vehicles. But the company has also spread around the world. Its models are built in Spain (by the subsidiary company, Motovespa, in Madrid), India (jointly with LML of Kampur), the People's Republic of China (by the joint venture of Piaggio Lyman Foshan), Taiwan (by the licensee Taiwan Vespa Company), Indonesia (by the licensee Danmotors), Thailand (by the licensee Thai Yarnion), Iran (by the licensee Sherkate Tolide), Pakistan (by the licensee Radija Industries), Tunisia, Egypt, Czech

Republic & Slovakia, Congo, and Venezuela. All of this in accordance that dates back to the beginning, when Piaggio understood right from the start that the miracle of Vespa would not find fertile soil only in Italy, but also in France, Germany, Belgium, Spain, and England. Working in those nations are license-holding companies such as the A.C.M.A. in Paris, Hoffman, Messerschmitt, M.I.S.A. in Brussels, and the Douglas company in Britain. And everywhere the result was the same, a success like that enjoyed in Italy. At the turn of the 21st century then, Vespa arrives with its full credentials to take a leap into the next millennium, ready to up the stakes on the bet it first made in long-ago 1946. Two-wheeled vehicles, and especially scooters, definitely have a great future before them. The chaotic traffic of the cities, the need to reduce pollution, the difficulties with parking, are all elements that realistically lead us to suppose that the old and lovable all-purpose Vespa of fifty years ago will continue, then, to accompany us, even in the coming fifty years....

THE PIAGGIO PLANT AT PONTEDERA (NEAR PISA) IS THE MOST IMPORTANT EUROPEAN CENTER OF MOTORCYCLE AND SCOOTER TECHNOLOGY. ITS MANUFACTURING FACILITIES CONSTITUTE A POINT OF REFERENCE FOR THE ENTIRE INDUSTRY. ABOVE, AERIAL PHOTOGRAPH OF THE COMPLEX, WHICH COVERS A TOTAL OF 600,000 SQUARE METERS.

50 **VESPA**

FIFTY YEARS HAVE PASSED SINCE THE FIRST PIAGGIO VESPA WAS PRESENTED TO THE PUBLIC, BUT IT IS EASY TO RECOGNIZE THE VERSION BEING MARKETED TODAY, THE GRANDCHILD OF THAT ORIGINAL MODEL: THE SAME GAZE, THE SAME EXPRESSION, THE SAME BODY. THE ONLY DIFFERENCE IS A SLIGHTLY MORE RAKISH CLOTHING SENSE, A TIGHTER OUTFIT THAT COMES IN MANY FUN COLORS. LIKE ITS GRANDMOTHER, IT HAS A CLASSIC NICKNAME, THE "CINQUANTINO," LITERALLY 'LITTLE FIFTY," GIVEN IT BY KIDS WHO WERE CERTAINLY THINKING OF THE ENGINE DISPLACEMENT, NOT THE HALF-CENTURY OF TRADITION THAT IT BEARS.

Engine: horizontal two-stroke single-cylinder, 49.8 cc. displacement, 2.3 hp, rotary-valve fuel injection, three/four-speed gearbox, lubrication with 2 percent mixture, top speed according to the Highway Code.

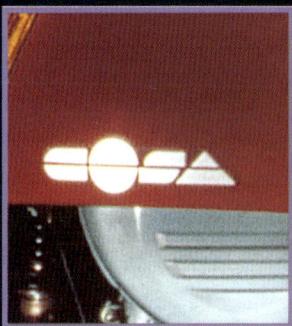

Engine: horizontal two-stroke single-cylinder, 125 cc., 150 cc., and 200 cc. displacement, electronic ignition, four-speed gear-box, lubrication with 6 percent mixture, top speeds of 92 kph, 95 kph, and 99 kph.

150 COSA

A "COSA," LITERALLY 'THING,' TO REPLACE THE VESPA? NOT EXACTLY... ACTUALLY... AN ALTERNATIVE VEHICLE, PERFECTLY SUITED TO CITY USE, STYLISTICALLY MORE ADVANCED, SOMETHING TO LINK THE PAST TO THE PRESENT BUT AT THE SAME TIME OFFERING A NEW AND EXCITING WAY TO THINK ABOUT THE VESPA. IN PRACTICE, THE NAME OFFERS ITSELF TO SOME AMUSING PUNS: IS THE 'THING" A VESPA? NOW, IS THE VESPA A 'THING,' OR A COSA? THE NEW NAME CAUSED NO REAL TROUBLE OR CONFUSION, AND WAS QUICKLY ACCEPTED INTO THE GREAT PIAGGIO FAMILY, REPRESENTING THE NATURAL EVOLUTION OF THE SPECIES...

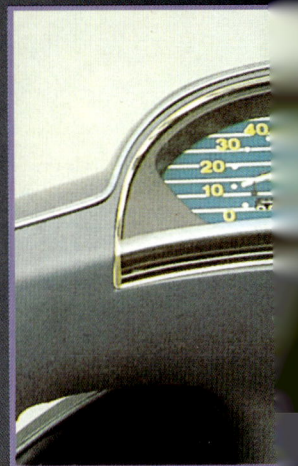

50
ZIP & ZIP

ZIP & ZIP IS THE PIAGGIO PRODUCT FOR THE YEAR 2000. THIS BIMODAL SCOOTER REPRESENTS THE FIRST APPLICATION OF THE COMPLETELY INDEPENDENT ELECTRICAL-PETROL PROPULSION SYSTEM APPLIED TO A PRODUCTION VEHICLE. THIS SOLUTION MAKES IT POSSIBLE TO USE THE INTERNAL COMBUSTION ENGINE ON THE WAY INTO THE CITY, WHILE THE ELECTRIC MOTOR CAN BE USED ONLY IN AREAS WITH SPECIAL ACCESS REQUIREMENTS. THE DIMENSIONS ARE THE SAME AS THE ZIP 50, FROM WHICH IT WAS DERIVED. THE BATTERIES ARE HOUSED UNDER THE SEAT AND THE PORTABLE BATTERY-CHARGER IS CONTAINED IN THE LUGGAGE COMPARTMENT IN THE FRONT SHIELD.

Bimodal scooter with two independent power plants: one electric (with a range of between 19 and 26 km.); the other internal combustion, two-stroke, 49.4 cc. displacement, using unleaded gas, top speed according to the Highway Code.

125
TYPHOON

THIS SCOOTER IS ALSO AN OFF-ROAD VEHICLE. AND WHY NOT? AFTER ALL, VESPA DID PLENTY MORE THAN THAT WHEN IT WAS SUMMONED TO THE FRONT, WHERE IT FACED COMBAT AND WON GLORY. CLEARLY, THAT EXPERIENCE TOUGHENED THE VESPA, BECAUSE THEY LED TO THE OFF-ROAD PERFORMANCE OF THE TYPHOON (MARKETED BY PIAGGIO UNDER THE GILERA TRADEMARK), RELAUNCHING AN OLD THEME DEAR TO THE "OLD" VESPA: TOURING (TURISMO). WITH THIS NEW SCOOTER, YOU CAN EASILY MAKE IT OUT TO THE COUNTRY FOR EXCURSIONS THAT WILL ALLOW YOU, FOR ONCE, TO ESCAPE CITY TRAFFIC.

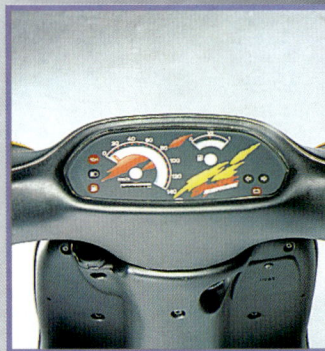

Engine: horizontal two-stroke single-cylinder, 123.5 cc. displacement, 13.8 hp at 7,750 rpm, Mikuni 20 carburetor, automatic transmission, unleaded gas, top speed 100 kph.

125 SFERA

"THE NEW CLASSIC SCOOTER": WITH THIS DEFINITION, PIAGGIO LAUNCHED THE "SFERA" IN 1990, THE FIRST SCOOTER THAT THE CASA DI PONTEDERA BUILT ENTIRELY OUT OF PLASTIC, AN ABSOLUTE NOVELTY WITHOUT PRECEDENTS. IT JOINS THE VESPA; IT IS NOT A FURTHER EVOLUTION OF THE VESPA, BUT A COMPLETE REINVENTION OF THE VESPA, MAKING THE BEST USE OF THE NEW MATERIALS NOW AVAILABLE. THE DESIGN, TOO, IS ALTERNATIVE, AND IS NICELY SUITED TO THE TASTES OF YOUNG PEOPLE. THE 1995 VERSION WAS EVEN MORE REFINED, CONFIRMING THE SUCCESS OF THE NEW LINE.

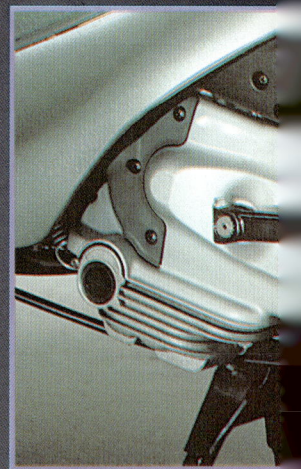

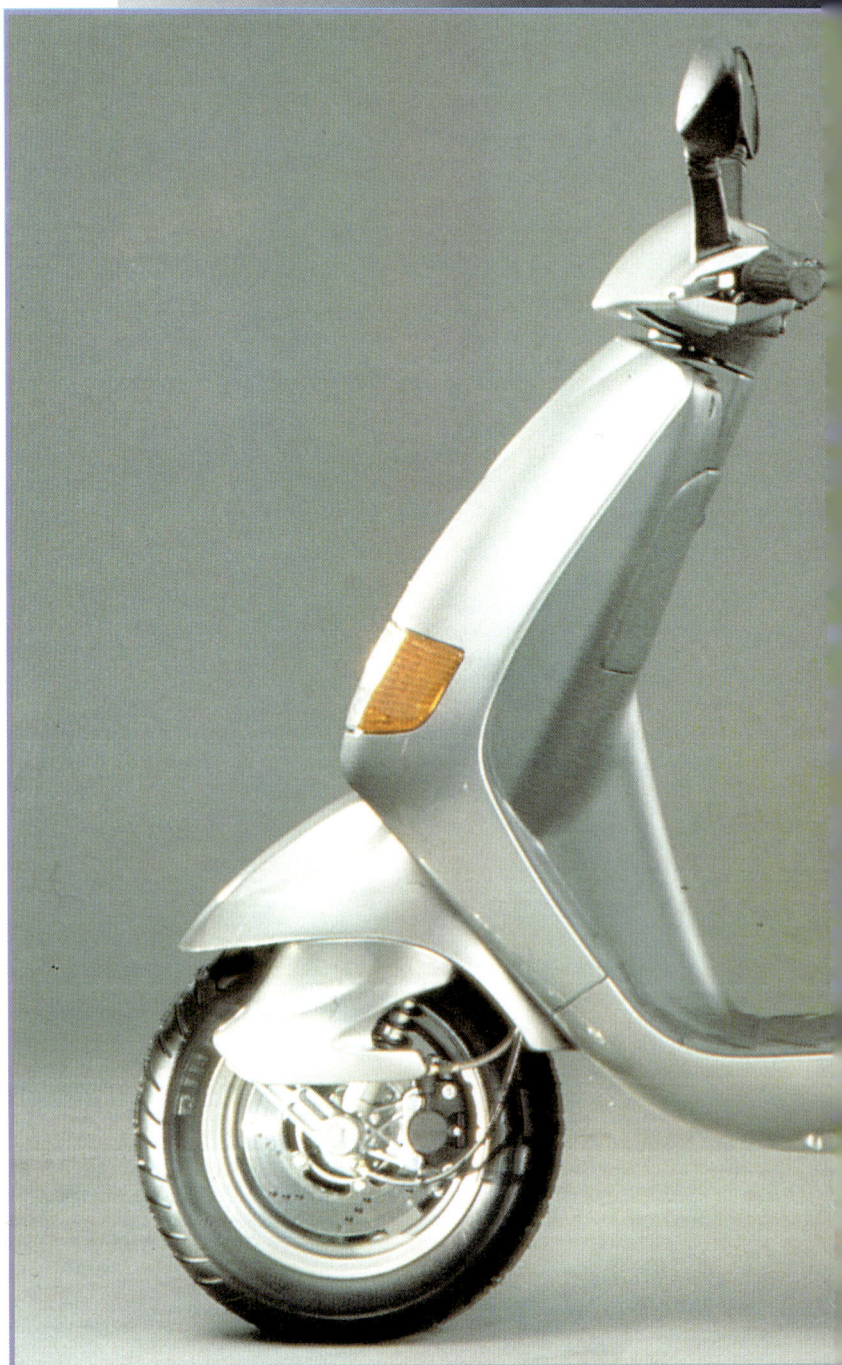

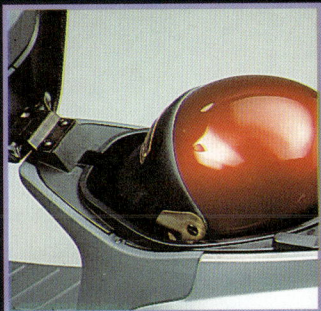

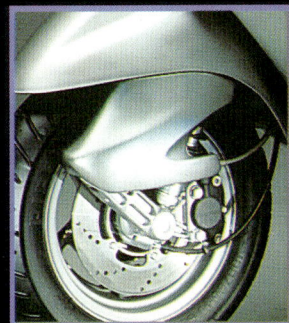

Engine: horizontal four-stroke single-cylinder, 124.2 cc. displacement, 12 hp at 7,750 rpm, Mikuni 24 carburetor, automatic transmission, unleaded gas, top speed 95 kph.

Engine: horizontal two-stroke single-cylinder, 123.5 cc. displacement, 14.4 hp at 7,500 rpm, Mikuni 20 mm. carburetor, automatic transmission, separate lubrication, top speed 105 kph.

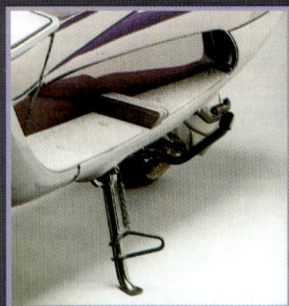

125 HEXAGON

This is a full-fledged a two-wheel mini-automobile for the city. The Hexagon boasted an enormously capacious luggage compartment perfectly integrated into the bodywork (with an interior courtesy light). With a very nice riding position that makes it possible to shift your feet the length of the running board and with an exceedingly comfortable and abundant saddle, this is certainly one of the most comfortable scooters in its category. Also note that in comparison with other "maxi-scooters," the Hexagon has a shorter wheelbase and remains eminently maneuverable in even the most intense traffic. Also available in a four-cycle 250 cc. version.

125 ET 4

CREATED IN 1996 TO CELEBRATE THE FIRST 50 YEARS OF VESPA. PIAGGIO COULDN'T HAVE FOUND A MORE THOUGHTFUL GIFT FOR ITS MANY ADMIRERS, WHO HAD ALWAYS DREAMED OF A SCOOTER WITH A METAL BODY SURROUNDED BY LOTS OF PLASTIC ACCESSORIES. THE RESULT WAS EXCEPTIONAL: A NEW AND UP-TO-DATE VESPA (WITH AUTOMATIC TRANSMISSION, FOUR-STROKE ENGINE, AND DISK BRAKES) THAT DID NOT FORGET THE PAST, STILL PRESENT IN MANY DETAILS. LAST BUT NOT LEAST, THE FLOWING SCRIPT NAME, HANDSOMELY ADORNING THE FRONT SHIELD.

Engine: horizontal four-stroke single-cylinder, 124.2 cc. displacement, 12 hp at 7,750 rpm, Dell'Orto 24 mm. carburetor, automatic transmission, unleaded gas, top speed 95 kph.

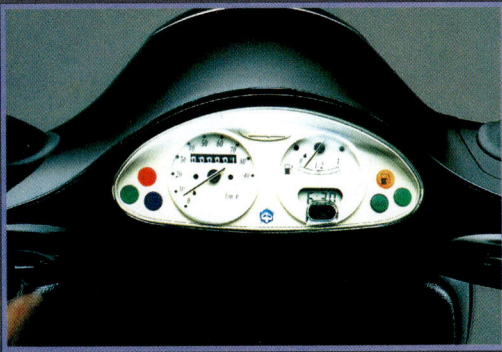

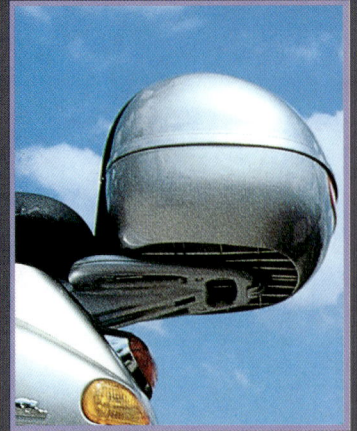

Engine: horizontal two-stroke single-cylinder, 49.3 cc. displacement, 4.5 hp at 5,700 rpm, Dell'Orto 11 mm. carburetor or else FAST direct fuel injection, automatic transmission, separate lubrication, top speed 45 kph.

ET2
50

50 ET 2

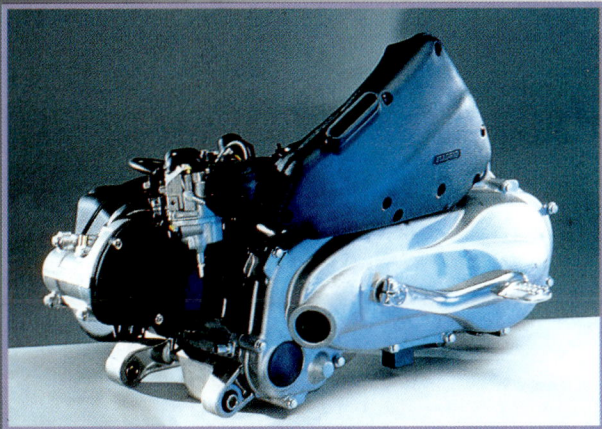

CREATED IN 1996 IMMEDIATELY FOLLOWING ITS BIG SISTER, THE ET 4, BUT THIS VERSION MAINTAINED THE TWO-CYCLE ENGINE. TO REDUCE THE POLLUTANTS IN THE EMISSIONS, HOWEVER, IT WAS ALSO OFFERED IN THE FAST VERSION, WHICH BOASTED ELECTRONIC FUEL INJECTION IN PLACE OF THE CARBURETOR, A GENUINE INNOVATION IN THOSE YEARS (NOTE PICTURE OF ENGINE, TOP). AND SO IT CONTINUED TO OFFER THE ADVANTAGES OF THE TWO-CYCLE ENGINE (LIGHTNESS, PERFORMANCE) WITHOUT THE SHORTCOMINGS (HIGH FUEL CONSUMPTION AND HIGH EMISSIONS).

GILERA

125 RUNNER

Half motorcycle and half scooter, the Runner represents a truly innovative idea. You climb on with your legs clamped around the centrla body, like on a motorcycle, but the small-radius wheels offer all the maneuverability of a scooter. It handles with particular precision, a factor that has not eluded the notice of the more performance-oriented young people, who can ride the 50 cc. version, while their older brothers and sisters can really go to town—or out of town—with the 180 cc. version.

Engine: horizontal two-stroke single-cylinder, 123.5 cc. displacement, 15 hp at 7,500 rpm, Mikuni 20 mm. carburetor, automatic transmission, separate lubrication, top speed 105 kph.

Peperino

Presented at the Munich automotive show in fall of 1998, the Peperino represented an interesting prototype. Alongside technical solutions that were reminiscent of the classic Vespa (such as front wheel-pull connecting rod suspension) there were avant-garde esthetic approaches, with a massive front-shield. But the most notable element was unquestionably the frame, which featured an extremely refined structure in pressure die-cast aluminum.

The legends

WHAT ARE VESPA ET4S DOING RECLINING ON PINK SHEETS, WADING IN THE TREVI FOUNTAIN, OR WALKING ON THE MOON? NOTHING. NOTHING NORMAL, CERTAINLY. QUITE SIMPLY, THEY ARE UNDERSCORING IN THE PIAGGIO ADVERTISING CAMPAIGN OF THE LATE NINETIES THE ALLURE OF THE MYTHS OF THE FIFTIES AND SIXTIES. THE PINK SHEETS HEARKEN BACK TO THE CLASSIC IMAGE OF MARILYN MONROE FROM THE FIRST EDITION OF "PLAYBOY" IN THE FIFTIES. THE SIXTIES FOR THE TREVI FOUNTAIN, AS IT APPEARED WITH ANITA EKBERG IN FEDERICO FELLINI'S "LA DOLCE VITA. AND THE SEVENTIES IN THE REMARKABLE MOONWALKS, BEGINNING WITH THE FIRST LANDING IN 1969.

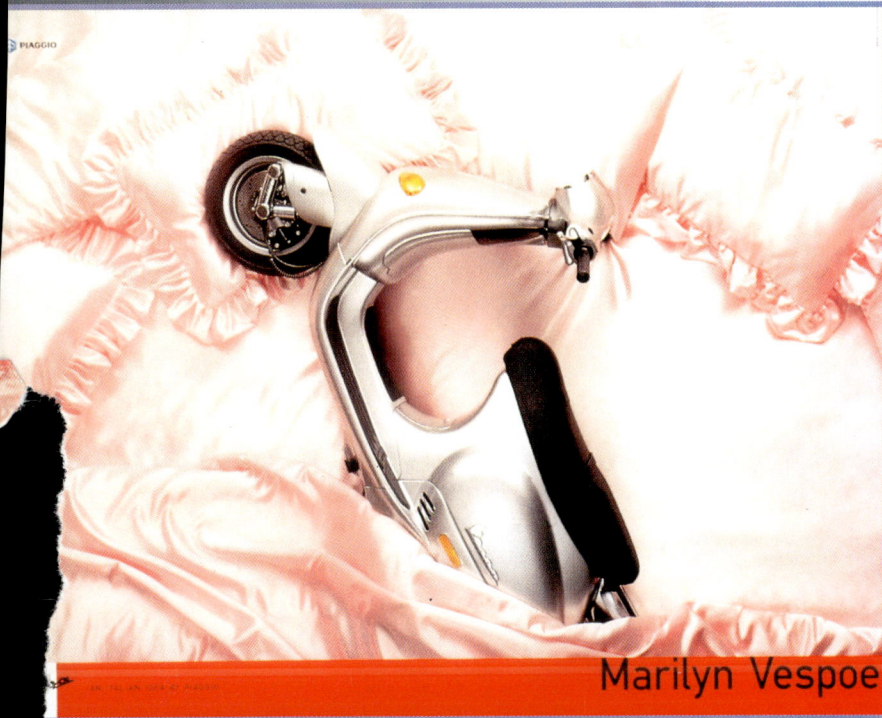

Marilyn Vespoe

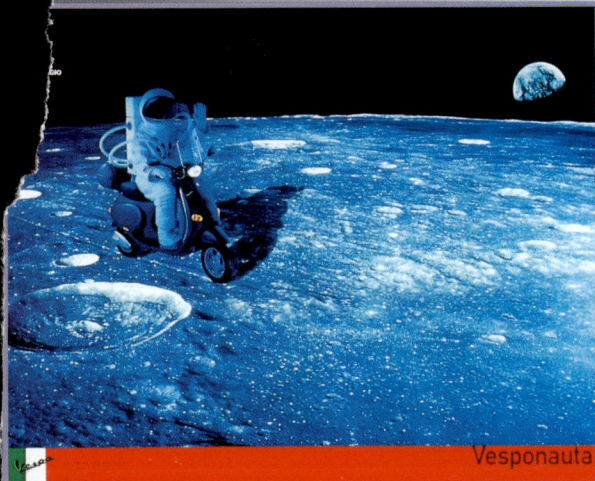

Vesponauta

La Dolce Vespa

127

Printed by
Arti Grafiche D'Auria of Ascoli Piceno
August, 2000